TI
BAPT
AC

2. 2.

You

BROADMAN PRESS • NASHVILLE, TENNESSEE

Credit: Jacket photograph—Baylor University

Dewey Decimal Classification: 267
Subject Heading: ASSOCIATIONAL WORK
Library of Congress Catalog Card Number: 78–73277
Printed in the United States of America

To Ruth

who too often has been taken for granted
and to whom too few words of appreciation have been spoken;
and to our daughters, Cindy and Nancy, who have brought joy
to our lives; and to the memory of our son, Norman,
who was taken to his eternal home at age sixteen,
but who will never be forgotten in our earthly home.

CONTENTS

PART III

The Association's Director of Missions

PREFACE

October, 1978

DEAR READER,

A friend read this in an earlier manuscript form and, being kind, said some nice things about it. He also suggested that I study *How to Read a Book*, by Mortimer Adler and Charles Van Doren. Apparently Bob thought my knowing how to read a book would help me to write one. I rushed to the library and read it the same day I received his letter. I hope my attempts to apply Adler's and Van Doren's suggestions to the final revision have made this book easier for you to read.

The authors of *How to Read a Book* said the reader should be able to state what the whole book is about with utmost brevity. I am going to do that now. This book is about the missionary outreach of Baptists—missionary outreach as it was implemented through, and usually initiated by, the association. It is about the association's premier role as an enabler in assisting Baptists, not only to move across the land geographically, but, also, to make inroads into the heart and fabric of both denominational and national existence.

Parts I and II combine to tell of the advance of Baptists, largely through the influences and activities of the associations, both *across* and *into* America. Part III then complements the first two by tracing the historical development of the office of the associational director of missions, something that I think has not been done previously by a Baptist writer.

Another thing Adler and Van Doren said you, dear Reader, should be able to do after having read a book is to enumerate its major parts, and to outline those parts as you should have outlined the whole. I am not going to explain that further nor do it here!

But I am going to point out that Part I, "The Association's Geographic Advance Across America," which consists of three chapters, describes the flow of Baptists, first, up and down the Eastern Seaboard, then westward to the Mississippi, and, finally, on to the Pacific. Chapter 1, "The Association and Baptists of Colonial America," briefly sketches associationalism's beginnings in England and Wales and then moves immediately to the organization of Philadelphia Association in 1707. An effort is made to explain how, and why, Baptists from Philadelphia, Charleston, and Sandy Creek associations had spread up and down the Atlantic from New England to Georgia before Lexington and Concord. The next chapter relates how Baptists joined the tide of migration that flowed irrevocably across the Alleghenies by means of that day's two main arteries of westward expansion—Boone's Wilderness Road and the Ohio River. The final chapter in Part I follows Baptists from the Mississippi Valley to Texas and, then, across plains, prairies, and mountains to California and the Oregon Territory.

Those who are interested in particular facets of Baptist life may find useful information in Part II. That part turns from geography to "The Association's Inward Advance into the Life of America." There are five chapters. "The Association's Developing Definition and Miscellaneous Influences" (chap. 4) contains historical materials that are not easily obtained elsewhere. After tracing the Baptist concept of autonomy, which largely determined associationalism's various definitions, seven miscellaneous, but very important, areas of influence on the denominational experience are explored briefly. Discipline, education, officers, ordinances, ordination, salary, slavery—all are reviewed historically in light of the minutes of hundreds of associational annual meetings. Most of those minutes were studied on microfilm bought from the Historical Commission or borrowed from the Fleming Library of Southwestern Baptist Theological Seminary and from the Baptist Historical Collection at Furman University. Reader, believe me when I say that five years of research, and pages upon top of pages of notes, went into the writing of that chapter.

Other chapters in Part II attempt to fill the void that has existed in Baptist history relative to the association's role. Take religious freedom, for instance. Isaac Backus, John Leland, Thomas Jefferson, James Madison, Roger Williams—all are recognized by most Baptists as having been important individuals in the struggle to gain freedom of religion. (Of course, I know I don't need to tell you that two of those gentlemen were not Baptists.) But few Baptists are aware of the fact that the Baptist association was the most important single institution in that fight—and that Backus and Leland served the cause of religious freedom entirely in an associational context. I kind of resent it that history, both Baptist and secular, has for the most part ignored the association's contributions.

Look at missions! The association has been front and center from the very beginning. I remember the guidon from those regimental parades I despised so during my army days. That's what the association has been in missions—the guidon leading the parade for the rest of the denomination! After all, when William Carey made his plea in 1792, it was made before a Baptist association. The scattered congregations (satellite) concept, salary supplements, supply of destitution, the itinerant missionary movement—really, Reader, the list goes on! All of those techniques of outreach and ministry are primarily the result of Baptist associational-ism. Indian missions! Shaftsbury Association showed the way to go—but just barely ahead of Charleston Association—shortly after the turn of the nineteenth century.

I think it's about time we gave the association a little respect!

By the way, my Indian chapter looks at the "Indian Problem" in a way that few Baptist writers have attempted previously. I'm speaking of that fast sketch that gives Indian history a once-over-lightly all the way from Columbus to Metacom and Roger Williams. Writing that chapter was presumptuous of me. But Frank Belvin read it and thought it should remain essentially as it is. And few people know more about Indians than does Indian Frank Belvin. Incidentally, the progress some Indian associations are making is reflected in the fact that the Muskogee, Seminole, and Wichita Indian Association sent Martha Kinney, who is one-quarter Seminole and three-quarters Creek, from Wewoka, Oklahoma, to Indio, California, as a missionary to our desert association this past summer.

The final chapter in Part II traces the woman's missionary movement as it evolved from the Female Mite and Cent societies that sprang up in the first decades of the nineteenth century until the SBC's Woman's Missionary Union was organized in 1888, and beyond to the present decade. The association was—and is—more than an interested spectator. It may have been on the sidelines at times; but it was never out of the game. As an associational director of missions, I'm glad that we were seating women at our annual associations before state and national conventions were, and, for that matter, before they were extended national suffrage.

Part III, "The Association's Director of Missions," may not hold everybody enthralled. But I think it belongs in the book. In fact, I think that part alone should make it worthwhile for every missionary. It should have been written years ago. Ben C. Fisher, as recently as 1975, called the directors of missions "one of the keys to Southern Baptist growth." I think that you will agree that at least one book ought to adequately delineate the historical development of the office occupied by so key a person. This book does that. The evolution of that office is traced through many missionary prototypes and sundry titles from South Wales in 1650 until the present date in America.

In reading over this letter, I'm not all that taken with it. Actually, I've thought of tearing it up. But, Reader, I wanted to point out some of the things to look for even before you read the book. Maybe I've done that. So I think I'll go ahead and mail it. By the way, in connection with what to look for, Adler and Van Doren said you should grasp the author's leading propositions by dealing with his most important sentences. I don't want to make too much of that. I just hope you can find mine! Besides, Rudolf Flesch would say that they are much too long!

Finally, dear Reader, I hope you will enjoy the book. And I hope to see you someday soon!

SINCERELY,

Elliott

ELLIOTT SMITH

P.S.: Don't forget the Index. Let's say you want to know about the role circular letters have played in Baptist life. Look in the Index. Every person and every major topic mentioned in the book is listed in the Index.

ACKNOWLEDGMENTS

Appreciation is due J. C. Bradley, Loyd Corder, and several others on the staff of the Home Mission Board who read the manuscript and made suggestions concerning it. Special gratitude is expressed to Jerry Graham of the Home Mission Board for the hours he spent with the manuscript. Many of his suggestions are reflected in the final copy. Appreciation is also extended to Meeler Markham who was at the Home Mission Board when the work was begun and who encouraged me to write it. Several others in different aspects of Baptist life read the manuscript, for which I am grateful.

The libraries of Golden Gate and Southwestern seminaries were gracious in sending materials, including both books and microfilm, for my research—as was the Baptist Historical Collection of Furman University Library.

I am grateful to Robert Hughes, Ralph Longshore, and others on the staff of The Southern Baptist General Convention of California, and especially to Elmer Gray, editor of *The California Southern Baptist.* Gratitude is also expressed to the churches, pastors, and friends I am privileged to serve as director of missions in Trinity Association on the desert of Southern California.

Finally, special appreciation is offered to Phyllis Sparkman, a longtime friend whom I had the joy of serving as pastor for five years, who struggled valiantly to remove my dangling participles.

PART I

THE ASSOCIATION'S GEOGRAPHIC ADVANCE ACROSS AMERICA

The Anabaptists in Pensylvania, resolving themselves into a Body, and determined to settle their principles in evry vacant Quarter, began to establish Meeting Houses also on the Borders . . . so that the Baptists are now the most numerous and formidable Body of People which the Church has to encounter with, in the Interior and Back Parts of the Province.

Charles Woodmason, 1765

The Reverend Charles Woodmason, itinerant Anglican minister to the Carolina backcountry in 1765, lifted up his eyes and looked on the fields—and saw Baptists!

Baptists were the subject of frequent laments in Woodmason's journal. To his dismay, not only had that brand of stubborn dissenters become "numerous and formidable," but, also, he complained, "The lower class chuse to resort to them rather than to hear a Well connected Discourse." He wrote to the Anglican Bishop of London in 1765, warning that "these Baptists have great prevalence and footing in North Carolina, and have taken such root there that it will require long time and pains to grub up the layers." On one occasion, he recorded in his journal, "Go where I will, I have half a dozen of these Wandering Stars (Separate Baptists) at my heels . . . . When I am departed, then they all fall to braying and discomposing Peoples Thoughts and Minds." On another occasion, he said that the Baptists were "continually ranging from River to River devouring the fastings of the land . . . . When one is gone, comes another and another . . . . Peoples Brains are turn'd and bewilder'd." His conclusion was that "had I an hundred Tongues, or as many pairs of legs, I could not singly oppose such a Numerous crew."[1]

The suddenness of the Baptist growth was suggested by another sentence from the suffering itinerant missionary's writings: "And yet twelve months past most of these People were very zealous members of our Church." He unwittingly stated what undoubtedly explained much of their swift spread across the Carolinas when he wrote, "You may depend that they'll bring Scripture for all that they assert." After several years of what appeared to have been a selfless, but futile, ministry in behalf of his Episcopal Church, Woodmason declared, seemingly in surrender to the Scripture-bringing Baptists, "I am determined to resign my commission as this next week to the Board of Church Commissioners."[2]

Although the frustrated Anglican missionary blamed the sorry state of his church's affairs in the Carolina backcountry on "Anabaptists in Pensylvania," an apparent reference to Baptists from Philadelphia Association, his aggravation could have been directed as accurately against Baptist associations nearer the scene. For Baptists from both Sandy Creek and Charleston associations were swarming across the Carolinas in the 1760s. In any case, Woodmason was right in attributing the phenomenal proliferation of Baptists in that decade to the entity in denominational life called the association. Before the end of 1767, there were six Baptist associations in Colonial America: Philadelphia, 1707; Charleston, 1751; Sandy Creek, 1758; Kehukee, 1765; Ketocton, 1766; and Warren, 1767. Most of them, but especially the first three, were extending missionary arms beyond their immediate areas.

And that is what this book is about—Baptists extending themselves in missionary outreach through associational action, from the first association founded in America at Philadelphia, and by those subsequently organized, until the present decade.

Such missionary outreach, as implemented through the association, is not a new subject for research, any more than it is a new activity in Baptist life. It has been treated in the past but usually as scattered bits and pieces of associational history interspersed between myriad other matters. Bits and pieces of extraneous matter will also intrude themselves into this work; for Baptist bodies do not function in isolation. But the focus will be on the Baptist association in history, with particular attention devoted to the association's contributions to Baptist life as the population increased and its center shifted ever westward. Baptist heritage is great, and the Baptist association contributed greatly to it.

Notes

1. Richard J. Hooker (ed.), *The Carolina Backcountry on the Eve of the Revolution* (Chapel Hill: University of North Carolina Press, 1953), pp. 20,80,92,109,111 (in the order quoted).
2. Ibid., pp. 112,109,111 (in the order quoted).

1.

THE ASSOCIATION
AND BAPTISTS OF COLONIAL AMERICA

Nay, Precious God, let light extend
To China and East India,
To Thee let all people band,
Who live in Wild America:
O let Thy blessed Gospel shine
That the blind heathen may be Thine.

Hymn by Benjamin Keach
about 1690

Those who write on the subject of Baptist associationalism must begin in England—even when the emphasis is on the association in America. Baptist historian Robert A. Baker paid tribute to that truth in the first paragraph of his published work, *The Southern Baptist Convention and Its People, 1607–1972.* "To understand Baptist beginnings in America," he wrote, "one must plant his feet in the soil of Great Britain." The first Baptists who influenced denominational development were either English or Welsh. The association itself, as a Baptist body, was of English origin.

There in England, at the dawning of the seventeenth century, Baptists emerged from whatever obscure past was theirs to become a recognizable denominational entity. They did so in an age that was fraught with change but which, at the same time, was euphoric in its optimism. For while the English were saddened by the death of Elizabeth in 1603, they exulted at their humbling of Spain's "Invincible" fleet fifteen years earlier. Their greatest moment thus far in world history had been recorded in 1588, and the challenge was to sail through new doors opened by that victory. Believing a world of wealth awaited their taking in exotic lands beyond the westward swells of the Atlantic, London's merchants were eager to claim their prosperous destiny. Even dissenters (which Baptists were) caught up in the day's euphoria indulged hopes that they too would share in the new golden age. Their dreams were dashed when James I, fresh from Protestant Scotland, pursued a policy that forced either conformity to the Church of England or flight from the land.

In the midst of those momentous times, Baptists began to distinguish themselves from other dissenters and find their own place in history. They did so through two separate streams that flowed from a single birthplace: London. One stream, the General Baptists, Arminian in theology, had minimal lasting significance to American Baptists. Some of that persuasion emigrated from England to the New World. They organized churches in Rhode Island during the last half of the seventeenth century and were found in Virginia by the second decade of the eighteenth. But by the time of the American Revolution, most colonial General Baptists either had switched affiliations or had succumbed to Deism and Unitarianism. Today, relatively few Baptists in America acknowledge General Baptist antecedents. However, millions claim to be in the spiritual lineage of the Particular Baptists, that other stream that also flowed from seventeenth-century London. Theologically Calvinistic, Particular Baptists emphatically stamped their imprint on Baptist history in America.

It can be argued that associationalism, which developed among both General and Particular Baptists, had its beginning when seven Particular Baptist churches gathered in London in 1644 and produced a written confession of their faith. For one thing, that document, which came to be called the London Confession of 1644, was the first confession of faith formulated by an associated body of Baptist churches. For another, from that date forward there would be little ambivalence among Baptists concerning either the proper candidate or mode of baptism. Further, the association that most historians do accord the honor of being first, Abingdon (usually referred to as Berkshire Association), which was founded in 1652, accepted the London Confession of 1644 as providing its churches with a common doctrinal basis which made association desirable.[1]

Regardless of what date is assigned to associationalism's birth, it is demonstrably true that the Baptist association, as an institution, has given continuity to the Baptist movement for more than three centuries. Such continuity is borne out by the fact that connectional links tied the first New World association at Philadelphia to earlier English and Welsh associations, which themselves were connected to those first London Particular Baptists. W. W. Barnes took note of associational continuity when he wrote: "Some of the immigrants to the colonies were Baptists from England, Wales, and Ireland. Familiar with the organized life in the old country, they soon introduced it into America, adopting the same terminology."[2]

Several practical inducements encouraged associationalism. The Puritan Revolution against the tyrannies of Charles I was in full flower when those seven Particular Baptist churches gathered to publish the London Confession of 1644. While victory for Oliver Cromwell's army, which included many Baptists, was virtually assured when Charles was defeated in July of that year at Marston Moor, victory for Baptists was less certain. Baptists feared, with reason, that whatever the outcome, they might still be considered illegal dissenters. Association of the small scattered congregations afforded a measure of mutual support, perhaps more moral than substantive.

However, as important as were the fellowship and moral encouragement gained from association, a more compelling reason for associationalism was to demonstrate Baptist orthodoxy. That becomes abundantly clear when one comprehends the message conveyed by the London Confession's title page.

The Confession of Faith, of those churches which are commonly (though falsely) called Anabaptists; presented to the view of all that fear God, to examine by the touchstone of the word of truth: as likewise for the taking off those aspersions which are frequently both in Pulpit and Print (although unjustly) cast upon them.[3]

The fledgling Baptist denomination desired that other Christians understand they were not of the radical antiestablishment persuasion typified by the early sixteenth-century Münsterites. Precisely that identification of Baptists with the most extreme of the Anabaptists was the one their tormentors delighted to make. In the same year the London Confession was published, Massachusetts Bay Colony characterized Baptists in essentially that way. The colony's ruling authorities outlawed Baptists and described them as being "incendiaries of common wealths and infectors of persons in main matters of religion and troublers of churches."[4] To counter that persistent image, the early associations produced confessions of faith in which they attempted to demonstrate their theological orthodoxy.

However, it was those purposes that developed later, and the functions which grew out of them, that justified the continued existence and spread of associations. *As associationalism came to flourish in America, from the founding of Philadelphia Association and on into the next century, one purpose, perhaps not primary at first, became more influential in shaping Baptist history than any other. That associational purpose was church growth and mission outreach.* Barnes noted that not only did associations serve as "Doctrinal Clearinghouses," but also as "effective agencies for the churches in missions."[5]

The Anglican missionary's lament in 1765 was an early, albeit unwitting, acknowledgment of how productive the Baptist association already had become as a missions catalyst. Thus, Bold Mission Thrust, centered as it has been in the association, is but a logical evolution of an outreach pattern that was established early in denominational history.

Philadelphia Association

How early that outreach pattern was established is reflected in the words of A. D. Gillette, as he described Philadelphia Association. "From its earliest history," he wrote, "it was forward in the work of Domestic Missions."[6] That was one of the association's cardinal characteristics. It was missionary almost from its birth. A. H. Newman declared, "No agency did so much for the solidifying and extension of the Baptist denomination in the American colonies as the Philadelphia Association."[7] William Cathcart's evaluation in 1881 was that the influence of that association "has been greater in shaping Baptist modes of thinking and working than any other body in existence."[8] Typically nineteenth century in their methods of presenting history, none of those historians were given to understatement. But if their conclusions were correct, the association's potential as an institution in Baptist life is pegged at a position of premier importance; and few other entities can challenge its preeminence in matters missionary.

The usual historical explanation is that five small congregations "in the Philadelphia area" came together in 1707 to form themselves into an association. Although the geography of that explanation is accurate, it is less than adequate. Only one of the founding churches, the Lower Dublin (interchangeably called Pennepek) Church, was in Pennsylvania; and none was in Philadelphia itself, then a town of some seven hundred houses. A Baptist congregation met in the Quaker City; but it was a satellite of the Lower Dublin Church. The churches which organized themselves into the first Baptist association in America were: Welsh Tract, which now is in Delaware; Cohansie; Middletown; and Piscatagua—to use Gillette's spelling—all in nearby West Jersey; and Lower Dublin, which was a few miles north of Philadelphia. Minutes preserved by the Lower Dublin Church described the historic event:

Before our general meeting at Philadelphia, in the seventh month, 1707, it was concluded by the several congregations of our brethren, such as they thought most capable in every congregation, and those to meet at the yearly meeting to consult about such things as were wanting in the churches, and to set them in order; and these brethren meeting at the said yearly meeting, which began the 27th day of the seventh month, on the seventh day of the week . . . .[9]

But the intent here is not so much to relate history as it is to define the nature and characteristics of America's first association of Baptist churches that caused it to be missionary, and having done that to suggest what, if any, carry-over there might be for missionary outreach today.

Doctrinal Soundness

The Anglican's complaint was right on target. Those Baptists who swept across the Carolinas and Virginia in the two decades before the Revolution brought Scripture for all they asserted. Philadelphia Association did not officially adopt its own confession of faith until one was approved in 1742, which was printed by a young man named Ben Franklin! But the Second London Confession, a Scripture-filled document drafted in 1677 and reaffirmed in 1689, was the churches' guide in those early decades.

Minutes of the annual meetings reveal how determined

the churches were to remain scripturally sound. One of the early meetings was confronted with a query sent to the association from the Cohansie Church. That congregation wanted to know "whether a pious person, of the number of Pedo-Baptists, who forbears to have his own children sprinkled, may be admitted to our communion without being baptized." It should be noted that a basic unanimity has prevailed among Baptists across the centuries concerning the ordinance of baptism. But it is also true that pesky differences in interpretation have continually plagued the denomination. In that instance, the answer was clear. It was "given to vote" by messengers to the association "and passed all in the negative." That is, the answer was no, unanimously no.

A church could not receive one who had not been immersed, regardless of how pious he might be. The shallow logic of a further question was also intelligently but tactfully refuted. The church wanted to know if refusing admittance to such a person did not "discover want of charity." The association responded: "It is not for want of charity that we thus answer. Our practice shows the contrary; for we baptize none but such as, in the judgment of charity, have grace, being unbaptized; but it is because we find in the commission that no unbaptized persons are to be admitted into church communion."

The significance of this event, which was recorded in the 1740 minutes of Philadelphia Association, was that the issue was resolved in accordance with what was found "in the commission." Responding to similar queries became an established practice in early American associationalism. As the associations formulated their scriptural answers, Baptist doctrine developed. Their almost total reliance upon the New Testament became one of the foundation stones upon which America's Baptists would build.

Denominational Continuity

Not only were the churches of the Philadelphia Association dedicated to biblical principles, but they were also committed to what might be termed denominational continuity. That commitment became a means both of preserving their Old World past and of propagating the gospel into the future.

Baptists had come to the friendly Quaker environs of the Jerseys and Pennsylvania in the latter decades of the seventeenth century. They brought with them their Particular Baptist beliefs and organizational backgrounds; and, as Newman phrased it, "Here . . . rooted themselves more firmly than in almost any other part of America, and here attained to a perfection of organization and to a degree of unity and uniformity in doctrine and polity that could be found no where else on the continent."[10] Newman also wrote: "The prevailing Welsh element among Pennsylvania Baptists had come from churches well grounded in an evangelical type of Calvinism and Baptist principles and practices. They combined evangelical zeal and fervor with a thorough-going denominational self-respect."[11] That statement is verified by minutes of the association where certain of its members were described as "some that had been ruling elders in the churches they came from . . . long concerned in affairs of churches and associations in their own countries."[12] Desire for continuity with the past became both their motivation and their means of spreading Baptist beliefs and practices.

That same denominational loyalty carried the Baptist message to colonial Virginia and the Carolinas and later to Georgia and across the Blue Ridge and beyond the Alleghenies to the Mississippi and Ohio valleys—and ever westward. That same loyalty would carry descendants of the first associations to Texas and would spread the Southern

Baptist witness from the Sabine to the Rocky Mountains and over them to the West Coast, first, prior to the Civil War and a second time during the dust-bowl days of the 1930s.

The desire for continuity with the past has been a major factor in the advance of Baptists across America, and it can continue to be. More than half of our states have fewer than one hundred Southern Baptist churches in them. Twenty-two of the states have fewer than fifty. Ten of the states have fewer than twenty.[13] While Southern Baptists ought never again to be content to colonize new-work areas, which being overly protective of the denomination tends toward, neither should they neglect a motivational factor that possesses so much potential for growth in many of those states.

Satellite (Scattered) Congregations

Their scriptural orientation and desire for denominational continuity gave the first Baptists of the Philadelphia Association the theological and emotional motivation for extension. Satellite congregations gave them their means. That was the only means of outreach available to them during the first decades of their existence.

When the eighteenth century began, the entire English population in America amounted to only 275,000.[14] Towns were small and scattered. Roads were few. Usually those were trails or wagon tracks marked uncertainly by notches cut into trees, and often were impassable. Add to those facts of eighteenth-century life the weak posture exhibited by Baptists as the era began. William G. McLoughlin estimated that "not more than one in one hundred persons in New England" was a Baptist when the eighteenth century got under way.[15] Most of those lived in Rhode Island. Outside of New England, except in the Charleston and Philadelphia areas, Baptists were hardly to be found. According to statistics provided by David Benedict (which were not always complete), there were only sixteen Baptist churches in all of the New World in 1700. That total included one Seventh-Day Church as well as First Baptist Church of Philadelphia, which did not officially organize as a separate congregation until 1746.[16] For Baptists, themselves still toddlers, to reach beyond their own Judeas approached the impossibility level.

But it was possible to reach "into the next towns." The fledgling churches of the Philadelphia Association did that. Newman explained how the satellite method, which was actually the scattered congregation technique of extension practiced by their ancestors in Wales the previous century, worked. He wrote: "These continued for some time to be members of the Pennepek (Lower Dublin) Church where they met from time to time to break bread, preaching services being held in each locality as often as convenient, while four quarterly meetings were held for evangelistic purposes at Burlington, Cohansey, Chester, and Philadelphia in rotation."[17] That the satellite method of extension resulted in new churches is demonstrated by the fact that several new congregations were added to the association during an age that was noted for its spiritual lethargy.

Without that satellite ministry in early eighteenth-century Philadelphia Association, it is doubtful that the next phase in mission outreach could have developed. The leaders of that next phase were being trained in the satellites of Philadelphia Association immediately prior to the Great Awakening. Newman wrote, "In the out-stations of the church brethren were raised up who could conduct the service to edification."[18] Some of them would heed calls that would lead them to Virginia and the Carolinas.

Outreach Beyond the Local Area

Missionary outreach moved into a more mature phase during the last half of the eighteenth century. The decade that began that century's last half got under way with one-and-a-quarter million Englishmen scattered across the thirteen colonies. At the time that comprised one fifth of the English-speaking world. Four communities—Boston, Charleston, New York, and Philadelphia—had grown beyond the village stage. However, most colonials still clung to coastal tidelands or clustered in villages huddled beside New England bays. The Blue Ridge was the western frontier, although the hardy, and foolhardy, were beginning to creep into the valleys beyond—to the increasing alarm of those valleys' ancient inhabitants. West of the Alleghenies, still virtually unexplored forests reached across the nations of the Iroquois League to the great Mississippi River.

That decade of the 1750s was one marked by memorable events. In retrospect, the year 1752 stands apart, indicative—at least symbolically—of what was to come in both American and Baptist life. It was the year that the Liberty Bell, which had been cast in England, was delivered to Philadelphia. Prophetically, it was inscribed with the biblical injunction of Leviticus 25:10 to "Proclaim liberty throughout all the land unto all the inhabitants thereof." Also in that year, on a blustery June day, the soon-to-be-famous grandson of Baptist Peter Foulger made his mark upon science. Benjamin Franklin, in his forty-sixth year, carried a kite and key through what one writer later described as "neatly patterned and tree lined streets . . . of Philadelphia with their rows of sedate, red brick and white trimmed houses."[19] In a pasture outside the Quaker City, Franklin sent the kite soaring into a thunderstorm and proved that lightning is a manifestation of electricity. His achievement received the plaudits of the intellectual world when the Royal Society of London awarded him the Copley Medal.

Philadelphia was the scene, or at least the point of departure, of yet another of 1752's noteworthy events, one that received no plaudits in that day and few in ours. That was the year when what now can be defined as a strategy of mission outreach beyond the local environs became the deliberate program of an association of American Baptist churches. Such was the far-reaching meaning when Philadelphia Association responded to appeals for help by sending John Gano, Benjamin Miller, Isaac Sutton, and John Thomas to Virginia.[20] From that year forward, "traveling preachers" would be on the road south. Minutes of the annual meeting of the association held October 8, 1754, record the results of those first bold-mission thrusts. The clerk recorded that the messengers "concluded to receive the church at Ketockton, and the church at Opekon, Virginia, into the fellowship of this association." That had been deliberate missionary outreach.

Other congregations formed. The association minutes of 1765 relate that it was "Agreed that the churches of Virginia have our leave to form themselves into an association, provided they go on the same plan and have union with us." Messengers from four churches gathered August 19, 1766, and organized the Ketocton Association, fifth such in the colonies. By 1772, it had grown to include thirteen churches totaling 1,150 members.[21]

It is unlikely such missionary extension, with its resultant growth, would have occurred had not doctrinally sound, denominationally minded brethren been "raised up" in the churches and satellites of Philadelphia Association. When the opportunity for advance had come, the association had been both ready and able to respond.

The Separate Baptists from Sandy Creek

Even as Philadelphia Association reached missionary arms southward, another army for Christ, then no larger than a man's hand, hovered beneath the horizon. It became the eighteenth century's "most significant event in North Carolina Baptist history." That is what the *Encyclopedia of Southern Baptists* called the founding of the Sandy Creek Church by Separate Baptists. Robert A. Baker broadened the significance by saying the South was "never the same" again.[22] One of America's foremost historians, Bernard Bailyn, even more universal in his appraisal, wrote: "These doctrinally self-conscious predestinarian evangelists of the eighteenth century . . . fiercely belligerent, acutely sensitive to slights, and indefatigable in righting every wrong done them . . . became the spearheads in the drive toward a fuller realization of equality."[23]

Shortly before the arrival of the first band of Separate Baptists at Sandy Creek, Governor James Glen of South Carolina heaped scorn upon the Piedmont "back settlers" to whom they would minister. "The parents in the back woods," he declared, after traveling among them, "come together without any previous ceremony," and then took the same "care in raising a litter of piggs" as in raising their numerous progeny, which were "equally naked and full as nasty." But the governor admitted an explanation for the paucity of Christian values among those backcountry settlers who presently would become objects of Separate Baptist zeal. "If the back settlers should wish to become Christians," he wrote, "they could not, for there was no clergyman within a hundred miles."[24]

Two years later those circumstances changed dramatically. Messengers to Philadelphia Association had been praying. "If you had heard the mournful complaints and requests of souls destitute of the means of the courts of God and his ordinances, sent to us from remote places, it would cause melting compassions in your hearts." So declared the associational minutes of 1750. The burden "for those who are like to perish" continued to grow, especially after missionaries were sent to Virginia in 1752 until, in 1755, the association was pleading that its constituents be "frequent at the throne of grace, that the Lord would send forth many faithful laborers into his vineyard." Philadelphia Association probably thought its prayers were answered when, as the minutes of 1755 related, "one ministering brother from the Jerseys, and one from Pennsylvania" were appointed to visit North Carolina with the association's "several churches to contribute to bear their expenses."

But God had already sent forth others. For Stearns & Company had already loaded their wagons with wives, children, and worldly goods and were headed south from Mill Creek, Virginia. They were bound for the crossroads in North Carolina called Sandy Creek. The Separate Baptist saga was on the road. It began more as a movement of migrants than as the march of a mighty Christian army.

They rattled into Sandy Creek in November 1755 and organized a church. There were sixteen members. Eight of them were named Stearns! The two leaders, Shubal Stearns and Daniel Marshall, were already fifty years of age and, also like many products of the Great Awakening, were recent converts from New England Congregationalism. It was not likely, in that winter of 1755, that a Baptist historian of the next century would write: "There are today probably thousands of churches that arose from the efforts of Shubal Stearns and the churches of Sandy Creek."[25] But that was William Cathcart's evaluation in 1881. Neither was it likely that Sandy Creek Separate Baptists ultimately would give character to much that defines Southern Baptists today. That they did is an undisputed fact.

The Carolina fields were white unto harvest for the Baptist message. Within three years, there were three churches and several hundred members. In January 1758, Sandy Creek, Abbott's Creek, and Deep River churches formed Sandy Creek association in order, said Stearns, "to impart stability, regularity, and uniformity to the whole."[26] Morgan Edwards, in a frequently quoted paragraph, summarized their success seventeen years after their arrival in North Carolina. He wrote:

Sandy Creek is the mother of all the Separate Baptists. From this Zion went forth the word, and great was the company of them that published it: it, in 17 years, has spread branches westward as far as the great river Mississippi; southward as far as Georgia; eastward to the sea and Chesapeake Bay; and northward to the waters of the Potomac; it . . . is become the mother, grandmother, and great-grandmother of 42 churches, from which sprang 125 ministers.[27]

Morgan Edwards' burst of enthusiasm caused him to overstate the case. A Separate Baptist movement existed in New England that was independent of Sandy Creek. To cite the most prominent example, Isaac Backus formed a Separate Baptist church at Middleboro, Massachusetts, in 1756, before Sandy Creek was out of the cradle. The progression from Congregational to Baptist, which occurred frequently, was reminiscent of the early seventeenth-century English experience when many of the first Baptists had moved successively from the Church of England to Puritan, then to Separatist and, finally, into the Baptist ranks. Backus began as "Old Light" Congregationalist, moved to "New Light" Congregationalist, then to the Separates, and ultimately arrived at the Baptist position. Entire bodies of New England Congregational churches traveled that route in the 1750s.

However, after Morgan Edwards' statement is properly qualified, there still is no diminishing the fact that when Sandy Creek Association grew from three churches in 1758 to forty-two in 1772, and 125 men had answered God's call to preach, it was one of the greatest outbursts of New-Testament Christianity the colonies had witnessed. Experiences fifty years later in the valleys of Kentucky, Tennessee, and Ohio would compare favorably. To a large degree those too would be extensions of the Separate Baptist movement.

Why did it happen? The answer to that question, along with the characteristics that caused Philadelphia Association to be missionary, is relevant to associationalism, in general, and to this quarter-century's bold-mission emphasis, in particular. Why were those Separate Baptists able to proliferate so rapidly?

Enthusiasm

M. A. Huggins has suggested that the Separate Baptists "had the fire and fervor of the Whitefield revival."[28] That fire, with its accompanying emotionalism, along with their habits and exaggerated mannerisms, made them what many would define today as having been the charismatics of Colonial America. That meant their detractors were legion. Enthusiasts, they were called. But the "braying," which Woodmason had scorned, reached the Carolina settlers whom he had described as living in "logg cabins like hogs," and whose "behaviour was as rude or more so than savages."[29] Woodmason characterized the roving teachers, which likely included many of those 125 Separate Baptist preachers, as being "a set of Rhapsodists, Enthusiasts, Bigots, Pedantic, illiterate, impudent, Hypocrites."[30] But the more vigorously they were attacked, the more enthusiastically the Separates preached and the faster they multiplied.

Shubal Stearns, the dominant figure among the Separate Baptists, and whose preaching was widely imitated, was described as being "magnetic in preaching powers," with "impressive tones" and "eyes that seemed to have had magical power." It was said further that "trembling, weeping, screaming, and catalepsy were common effects of his highly impassioned exhortations."[31] Such extreme manifestations caused not only the Episcopalians but even other Baptists to find them to be objectionable. Robert A. Baker wrote: "The zeal and emotional preaching of the Separates, the use of uneducated ministers, the noisy meetings, and even the extensive ministry of women in the services alienated the more formal older Baptists."[32] But by the close of the Revolutionary War, the Separate Baptists had moved toward the middle of the road and, within two decades afterward, had united with Regular Baptists.

Persistence

In addition to their enthusiasm, the Separate Baptists of Sandy Creek possessed a stubbornness that defied both description and their oppressors. They and Regular Baptists were persecuted systematically in Virginia, even up to the very eve of the Revolution. Six weeks after the Boston Tea Party, James Madison wrote to a friend:

That diabolical Hell conceived principle of persecution rages among some and to their eternal infamy the clergy can furnish their quota of imps for such business. . . . There are in the adjacent county not less than 5 or 6 well meaning men in close gaol for publishing their religious sentiments which in the main are very orthodox.[33]

Craig, Ireland, and Waller—and many others—could authenticate the accuracy of Madison's insight.

The Baptist response to oppression was rapid growth. Garnett Ryland wrote that Baptist churches were formed in every Virginia county where Baptists were imprisoned.[34] Another observer of the times remarked that "the persecutors found that the imprisonment of preachers tended rather to the furtherance of the Gospel."[35] When fifteen hundred families were driven from Sandy Creek Association as an aftermath of the Battle of Alamance, Sandy Creek was decimated; but new churches sprang up where the persecuted found refuge. Many fled to Kentucky-Tennessee, thus spreading the Separate Baptist message to the western frontier.

Evangelism

That was the name of the game. Separate Baptists were ardently evangelistic. Reuben E. Alley wrote: "Those who committed themselves under this experience promptly received evidence of God's pleasure by seeking the salvation of men. True commitment required a person to be an evangelist for Christ."[36] Virginians, disillusioned with the vices and worldliness of the established clergy, warmly received that evangelistic message.

Second-generation Separate Baptists, who migrated in masses from the Carolinas and Virginia to the western frontier after 1790, were still "seeking the salvation of men." Their descendants, both spiritual and actual, are scattered throughout the Southern Baptist Convention today. Evangelism is still the name of the game.

The Annual Meeting

In the eighteenth century, and especially in Sandy Creek Association, the annual meeting often was an instrument of extension. In a book published more than 125 years ago, David Benedict explained how the annual associational meeting became a means of mission outreach. Speaking of the far-flung Sandy Creek Association, he wrote:

By means of these meetings, the gospel was carried into many new places. . . . Many became enamored with these extraordinary people, and petitioned the association to send preachers into their neighborhoods. These petitions were readily granted, and the preachers as readily complied with these appointments.[37]

The importance of the annual meeting was further emphasized by the statement, "These things so inflamed the hearts of the ministers, that they would leave the association with a zeal and courage which no common obstacle could impede." One of the participants described the scene as follows:

We continued together three or four days. Great crowds of people attended, mostly through curiosity. The great power of God was among us. The preaching every day seemed to be attended with God's blessing. We carried on our association with sweet decorum and fellowship to the end. Then we took leave of one another, with many solemn charges from our reverend old father, Shubal Stearns, to stand fast unto the end.[38]

Sandy Creek Association had grown to the extent that in 1770, at the annual meeting held at Grassy Creek, it was agreed to divide it into three bodies. Also complaints had surfaced that Shubal Stearns and the association exercised undue authority over the churches. The rationalization used to justify usurpation of local church authority was "that though complete power be in every church, yet every church can transfer it to an association."[39] The result was that three associations organized according to geography. North Carolina churches remained in the association which retained the original Sandy Creek name. Congaree Association was established for churches in South Carolina. Those in Virginia belonged to the General Association of Separate Baptists, which, along with New England's Warren Association, became the most influential association in the final surge toward religious freedom.

Churches of those associations joined other Baptist congregations (which totaled 457 as the colonial period drew to a close) in pressing the claims of the gospel upon a people who were hurrying toward Lexington and Concord.[40] Westward migration and further missionary extension must await the conclusion of that coming conflict. But Baptists would not be a disinterested people. Their concern was voiced in the October 15 session of the 1776 annual meeting of Philadelphia Association:

This association, taking into consideration the awful impending calamities of these times, and deeply impressed with a sense of our duty to humble ourselves before God, by acknowledging our manifold sins, and imploring his pardon and interposition in favor of our distressed country and also to beseech him to grant, that such blessings may accompany the means of his grace that a revival of pure and undefiled religion may universally prevail.

Notes

1. B. R. White (ed.), *Association Records of the Particular Baptists of England, Wales, and Ireland to 1660* (London: The Baptist Historical Society, 1971), "Abingdon Association," p. 125.

2. William Wright Barnes, *The Southern Baptist Convention: A study in the development of Ecclesiology* (Seminary Hill: Published by the author, 1934), p. 14.

3. W. J. McGlothlin, *Baptist Confessions of Faith* (Philadelphia: American Baptist Publication Society, 1911), p. 171.

4. Nathaniel B. Shurtleff, *Records of The Governors and Company of The Massachusetts Bay in New England* (Boston: From the press of William White, 1853), vol. 2, p. 85.

5. Barnes, p. 16.

6. A. D. Gillette (ed.), *Minutes of Philadelphia Baptist Association, 1707–1807* (microfilm copy obtained from the Historical Commission, SBC), Preface.

7. A. H. Newman, *A History of The Baptist Churches in the United States* (New York: The Christian Literature Company, 1898), p. 210.

8. William Cathcart, *The Baptist Encyclopedia* (Philadelphia: Louis H. Everts, 1881), vol. 2, p. 917.

9. Gillette, Philadelphia Association, p. 25.

10. Newman, p. 200.

11. Ibid., p. 210.

12. Gillette, Philadelphia Association, p. 25.

13. *The Quarterly Review*, vol. 37, no. 4 (July, August, September, 1977), p. 15.

14. Gordon Carruth (ed.), *The Encyclopedia of American Facts & Dates* (New York: Thomas Y. Crowell Company, 1970), p. 38.

15. William G. McLoughlin, *New England Dissent, 1630–1833:* The Baptists and Separation of Church and State (Cambridge: Harvard University Press, 1971), vol. 1, p. 9–10.

16. David Benedict, *A General History of the Baptist Denomination in America and Other Parts of the World* (New York: Lewis Colby and Company, 1848), pp. 364–65.

17. Newman, p. 202.

18. Ibid., p. 203.

19. Merrill D. Peterson (ed.), *The Founding Fathers: James Madison, A Biography in His Own Words* (New York: Harper & Row, 1974), p. 45. The portion quoted describes the city as it appeared in September 1774.

20. John Gano, *Biographical Memoirs of the Late Rev. John Gano of Frankfort,* formerly of the City of New York, written principally by himself (New York: Southwicke and Hardcastle, 1806, pp. 39–41). And Robert A. Baker, *The Southern Baptist Convention and Its People, 1607–1972* (Nashville: Broadman Press, 1974), p. 43. There is some difficulty in establishing the date of Gano's first missionary journey. He is listed as a delegate to Philadelphia Association for the first time in 1752. However, the minutes of the annual meetings do not establish when the first mission occurred. His memoirs were written fifty years after the event. From subsequent associational records, and from counting back from events that occurred after the journey, 1752 appears to be the most likely date.

21. Baker, p. 45.

22. Ibid., p. 49.

23. Bernard Bailyn, *The Ideological Origins of the American Revolution* (Cambridge: Harvard University Press, 1967), p. 261.

24. Richard J. Hooker (ed.), *The Carolina Backcountry on the Eve of the Revolution* (Chapel Hill: University of North Carolina Press, 1953), Intro., XXV.

25. Cathcart, p. 1099.

26. As quoted in Baker, p. 50.

27. Ibid.

28. M. A. Huggins, *A History of North Carolina Baptists, 1727–1932* (Raleigh: The General Board, Baptist State Convention of North Carolina, 1967), p. 51.

29. Hooker, p. 7.

30. Ibid., p. 42.

31. Newman, p. 293.

32. Baker, p. 49.

33. Peterson, p. 29.

34. Garnett Ryland, *The Baptists of Virginia, 1699–1926* (Richmond: The Virginia Baptist Board of Missions and Education, 1955), pp. 85–86.

35. Robert B. Semple, *A History of the Rise and Progress of Baptists in Virginia* (Richmond: Pitt & Dickinson, 1894), p. 45.

36. Reuben Edward Alley, *A History of Baptists in Virginia* (Richmond: Virginia Baptist General Board, 1974), p. 36.

37. Benedict, p. 685.

38. Ibid.

39. Baker, quoting Benedict, p. 51.

41

40. The figure of 457 Baptist churches is found in the Special 1776 issue of *Time*, r 51. Other sources give slightly different statistics. William Warren Sweet, *The Story of Religion in America* (New York: Harper & Bros., 1930), pp. 172–73, gives the statistics relative to the number of churches at the close of the colonial period as follows: Congregational, 658; Presbyterian, 543; Baptist, 480; Quakers, 295; German and Dutch Reformed, 251; Lutheran, 151; Catholic, 50; Methodist circuits, 37.

2.

THE ASSOCIATION AND THE MIGRATION OF BAPTISTS TO THE MISSISSIPPI

Part of the several Baptist Churches in the Illinois met at Anthony Badgleys on friday the 9th of January 1807 & having there agreed to Strive to gain a fellowship with each other Apointed two members out of each Church to bring the dsign into effect, we the Committee met at brother David Badgleys & Proceeded to business, brother Wm Jones Moderator, we the Committee agree to unite on the following principles-

Minutes of the Organizational Meeting Illinois Association of Baptists, 1807

Although cessation of hostilities was not declared officially until 1783, the Revolutionary War ended in essence on October 19, 1781, when Cornwallis surrendered his hopelessly surrounded British army at Yorktown, Virginia. Americans began to look longingly beyond the westward mountains again. Baptists looked and moved with the rest.

Some had not awaited the end of the war. Even as Philadelphia Association gathered for a daybreak prayer meeting six days after Yorktown to rejoice at the "signal success granted to the American arms,"[1] Lewis Craig and most of his Spottsylvania congregation were already strung out along Boone's Wilderness Road, "goin' to Kaintuck." Perhaps to Craig's surprise, when they arrived on Gilbert's

Creek late in 1781, they discovered that Baptists were already in Kentucky. Others had made the trek before them. Thousands more would follow. One writer on the subject of Baptist expansion into the West estimated that, in the two decades from 1791 to 1810, one fourth of the Baptists in Virginia migrated to Kentucky.[2] Supporting statistics suggested that, of the 75,000 people living in Kentucky in 1790, 90 percent had arrived by way of the Wilderness Road, which was the usual route taken to the frontier by Virginians.

What became a swollen stream in the decade following Yorktown had been a trickle even before the Revolution. The drift of settlers south from Pennsylvania down the Great Valley of Virginia, which had begun to reach tentacles down the western slopes of the Alleghenies, had been stopped, temporarily, in the 1750s by the outbreak of the French and Indian War. Philadelphia Association's minutes of 1754 reveal that a day of prayer was set for November of that year "in consequence of . . . the imminent danger our continent labors under, from the bold encroachments of our avowed enemies on our frontiers." Nevertheless, the bold encroachments continued, and, the next year, Indian pressure forced the Opekon Church to move back across the Shenandoah to the eastern side of the Blue Ridge where, for two years, it met with the Ketocton Church. Renewal of westward migration, following that war's successful conclusion for England and her colonies, was slowed a second time by the Proclamation of 1763. That unpopular decree, which was an effort of English authorities to placate Chief Pontiac who had led a bloody rebellion on the western frontier, established a line along the Alleghenies beyond which the colonies were not permitted to expand.

However, it took more than the Great Seal of England impressed upon a proclamation to prevent, for long, a movement as inevitable as was the westward migration. Given the Americans inconsequential regard for rights guaranteed to Indians by treaty, there was no chance anything as arbitrary as was the Proclamation Line could halt for long the movement beyond the mountains into the lush valleys of the Mississippi River system. That westward flowing tide was as irrevocable as the sun's arc across the heavens. As Lord Grenville, the Proclamation Line's chief proponent, was to discover on other occasions, what was proclaimed in London did not necessarily produce in America.

A foremost historian of the westward expansion declared that by 1763 the more adventurous of the pioneers were poised atop the Appalachians; and he added: "During the next dozen years, frontiersmen assaulted that wilderness so successfully that by the time of the Revolution their lonely cabins dotted the lowlands about the Forks of the Ohio, the bluegrass regions of Kentucky, and the winding valleys of the upper Tennessee River."[3] It is known that some of those cabins in Kentucky, and along the banks of the Wautauga and Holston in Tennessee, were raised by Baptists who had been schooled in the rigid ways of Shubal Stearns and the Separate Baptists of Sandy Creek Association.

Daniel Boone came to symbolize the pioneering spirit that characterized those early explorers who were rugged individualists before the cliché became one. Although he was not the earliest, and his exploits were not the greatest, he was the one who caught the world's fancy. Lord Byron, in seven stanzas of praise contained in *Don Juan*, extolled Boone while picturing his forest life as being one of pristine sinlessness.[4] However, the real Daniel Boone was a wanderer who continued to look over the next mountain as long as he lived. He was a "long hunter" who, on one occasion, engaged in a hunt and exploration that kept him away from his family on the Yadkin for a two-year stint. The long hunters of that century became the mountain men of the next who left the Mississippi in search of streams called Snake and Platte. They were wanderers who were always moving farther west until there was no west farther. Such adventurers are important to the initial development of a territory. But Daniel Boones do not build churches.

Neither do Squire Boones. Several historians have commented that Squire Boone, Daniel's less renowned brother, was a Baptist preacher who may have conducted some of his denomination's first services on the Kentucky-Tennessee frontier. Perhaps so. But it is also certainly true that Squire Boone's preaching seldom interfered with his hunting and exploring with Daniel. Much more is recorded of his recreation than of his worship. One must look elsewhere for the beginning of a meaningful Baptist witness on the new frontier.

Prohibitions to settling west of the Proclamation Line were removed in 1768. The westward trickle became a flood. One observer on Pennsylvania's western border wrote in 1770, "All this spring and summer, the roads have been lined with waggons moving to Ohio."[5] Concurrently, eastern Tennessee received its first sizable influx of settlers from North Carolina and Virginia. Hundreds of them were Separate Baptists who were fleeing from Sandy Creek Association following the Battle of Alamance to avoid the persecution practiced against them by Governor Tryon who called them "enemies of society and a scandal to common sense."[6]

Early Baptist work, which was organized after the Separate Baptists arrived in Tennessee from North Carolina, was dissipated by Indian activity incited by Tory agitation during the first years of the Revolution. But by 1779, although still a war year, the situation had stabilized sufficiently for the Buffalo Ridge church, credited with being first in Tennessee, to organize on Boone's Creek under the leadership of Tidence Lane, a family name honored in Separate Baptist history.[7] Before the surrender of Cornwallis, several Baptist churches had been founded in East Tennessee, and met semiannually in the fashion of an association. Choosing to consider themselves an extension of Sandy Creek, they submitted reports to the mother association for approval. Thus the evangelism and missionary outreach of Sandy Creek Association, which had scattered Baptists up and down the Atlantic from New England to Georgia, had, before 1780, extended the Baptist witness to Tennessee.

There had also been tentative movements by Baptists into Kentucky during the war. Thomas Tinsley was conducting Baptist worship services at Harrodsburg in 1776. Baptists were among many who migrated from Virginia in 1779. Joseph Barnett, John Whitaker, and John Gerrard—all from Virginia—led in founding the Severns Valley Church in June, 1781.[8] That work has continued across the decades and, with the same name, exists today as a Southern Baptist congregation in Elizabethtown, Kentucky. At the same time the Severns Valley Church was being organized, Craig's soon-to-be "Travelling Church" was packing in Virginia for its long trek to the frontier. They arrived on Gilbert's Creek late in 1781 where, on the second Sunday in December, they gathered for worship "around the same old Bible they had used in Spottsylvania."[9]

It was after the war that the movement west became an avalanche. As is often the case, hard times followed the war; in fact, hard times had dogged Americans throughout the conflict. Many Baptists, and others who shared their general class as the economically underprivileged, looked to cheap land and a new start beyond the mountains for their deliverance. The result was that all the available routes to the Kentucky-Tennessee-Ohio frontier were soon choked with people. Several routes existed. From the middle states, settlers moving west came down the Great Valley Road, which, known in earlier centuries as the Great Indian War-path, had been beaten out by the footprints of the ages. At Fort Chissel (sometimes Chiswell) in southwestern Virginia, they were joined by travelers who followed a feeder road across Flower Gap from the Carolinas. West from there it turned into Boone's Wilderness Road. Settlers going west from states north of Virginia often took Braddock's Road from Fort Cumberland across Pennsylvania to Fort Pitt (Pittsburg) from where they floated down the Ohio River to the frontier.

The magnitude to which the migration had grown within a few years after the war is illustrated by an army inventory of people, animals, and equipment that moved down the Ohio. From June 1 to December 9, 1787, a total of 146 boats floated down the river carrying 3,196 persons, 1,381 horses, 171 cattle, 245 sheep, 24 hogs, and 165 wagons.[10]

One of those statistics was a short, corpulent in his sixtieth year, Baptist preacher named John Gano. If Daniel Boone stands as a symbol for adventuresome frontiersmen whose explorations opened the valleys of Kentucky and Tennessee for westward expansion, John Gano stands in the same capacity for those selfless preachers who pioneered the way for Baptists to spread across nineteenth-century America. When Gano was born at Hopewell, New Jersey, on the eve of the Great Awakening, fewer than 600,000 people lived in the American colonies. All but a tiny portion of those dwelled east of the Blue Ridge in a narrow band that extended from Charleston to Boston. The leading city was Boston with a population of 12,000. Philadelphia was in close pursuit with 10,000 followed by New York which had a population of 7,000. Charleston, South Carolina, had a population of 3,500.[11] Early Baptist historian, David Benedict, reported that there were only thirty-two Baptist churches in America at the time.[12] (His statistics did not include the General Baptist churches which must have existed in Virginia and North Carolina.) Of those thirty-two, with the single exception of the church at Charleston, all were clustered in either New England or in the Middle Colonies where they formed an arc around Philadelphia. No Particular Baptist church existed in Virginia or North Carolina when Gano was born in 1727.

Before John Gano died in 1804 at Frankfort, Kentucky, that oft-times itinerant preacher of Philadelphia Association had seen his country grow from thirteen English colonies to seventeen United States which reached westward from the Atlantic to the Mississippi. During the seventy-seven eventful years of his life, the population had grown to approximately 6,000,000. Baptist ranks had swollen to well over 2,000 churches with almost 200,000 members.[13]

John Gano's name first appeared in the minutes of Philadelphia Association in 1752 when he was a young man of twenty-five. He quickly became the association's foremost itinerant missionary. In the mid-1750s, in what was a joint venture of Charleston and Philadelphia associations, he and his new wife went to the Yadkin River area of North Carolina where young Daniel Boone was one of the "back settlers." The Ganos stayed on the Yadkin until the Cherokees forced their departure at the height of the French and Indian War. In 1762, he became pastor of the First Baptist Church of New York City, itself a significant extension of Baptist work. Gano remained with the New York church for twenty-five years, except that for eight of those years he was on leave to serve as a chaplain to the Colonial forces. He was one of that band of Baptist chaplains that Washington later described as having been "the most prominent and useful in the army." When the cessation of hostilities was proclaimed at Washington's headquarters in 1783, he was the chaplain chosen to voice the prayer.[14]

The peacetime year of 1784 found Gano back with his Baptist brethren at the annual meeting of Philadelphia Association. He was selected to write the circular letter. In 1786, he preached to the association from 1 Timothy 4:1. Then, suddenly, in 1788, the church letter of First Baptist Church of New York City reported a new pastor. John Gano had been counted among the 3,196 persons who floated down the Ohio between June 1 and December 9, 1787. He had "gone to Kaintuck."

Gano's years of service in Philadelphia Association, where he had attended at least sixteen annual meetings and had been moderator three separate terms, plus his wartime fame and outstanding preaching ability, brought him immediate acceptance as a leader of young Elkhorn Baptist Association. When he arrived at his first annual meeting in 1788 as the sixty-one-year-old pastor of Lexington's Town Fork Church, he was chosen moderator. Accepted as an instant authority in things Baptist on the frontier, he administered his position of honor with grace and a rare wit.

But Gano was the exception rather than the rule. Most frontier preachers were of the lesser educated Separate Baptist origins. William Warren Sweet made the statement that "of the first twenty-five Baptist ministers in Kentucky, twenty were known to have been Separate Baptists in Virginia or North Carolina."[15] Most had been called from plowing to preaching or, more likely, to plowing and preaching.

Walter Brownlow Posey described the frontier preacher. He wrote: "He wore the common garb of his fellow citizens. His face was bronzed by exposure, his eye had a piercing glance, and his voice rang with a melting tone." A critic remarked, less appreciatively, "Hardly any of them looked like any other people." What a frontier preacher sometimes did with and to a text would break up a congregation today. Posey cited several examples. One preacher, preaching from the apostle Peter's admonition to "Gird up the loins of your mind," mistook loins for lines, and sermonized: "There are various kinds of lines—lines by which carpenters execute their work—lines for the division of land—lines of stages for travellers—lines for guiding unruly teams." Another explained that "Save yourself from this untoward generation" was a warning to "untowered" people who possessed no tower of refuge. Still another, in what might be appropriate for twentieth-century election years, misinterpreted "Perilous times shall come" as "Politious times shall come." Instead of being brought up at the feet of Gamaliel, Paul was brought up at the foot of Gammel Hill, which was so poor it wouldn't sprout peas, and so Paul had to get a job making tents. Perhaps topping all others was the unique message one preacher shared from Habakkuk 3:2, "Revive thy work in the midst of the years." He proceeded to enlighten his congregation: "Now that's where the work begins, but does not stop." Grasping his ears, he continued, "Right between the two years, right in the middle of the mind, and from the midst of the two years, it goes down to the heart."[16]

"Heartfelt" preaching was effective on the frontier. In a sense, it was the North Carolina Separate Baptist story of the previous generation being rewritten. The very lack of ministerial education often was an asset. Frontiersmen lived in an intensely emotional environment. They did things with abandon. Gouging was a popular sport, and drinking hard liquor was a popular pastime. Such folk would rather start in the midst of the years, and go down to the heart than to sit through "a well connected discourse." Those transplanted Separate Baptist preachers were on target, perfectly "on mission in their setting."

By the time of John Gano's death in 1804, Baptist work was firmly established in Kentucky and Tennessee. As has already been noted, the Severns Valley church had organized in 1781, and Craig's Spottsylvania church gathered on Gilbert's Creek in Kentucky around its "same old Bible" in the same year. Associational development followed quickly. Yearning for the same organizational structures to which they had been accustomed back east, messengers from six churches formed the Elkhorn Baptist Association at the home of John Craig on Clear Creek in 1785. It was the first association to be organized west of the Alleghenies. A month later, four other small isolated churches sent messengers to Cox's Creek to organize Salem Association. In 1786, survivors from Sandy Creek, who until then had maintained their affiliation with the mother association, finally declared an amiable separation and founded Holston Association in Tennessee. Seven churches constituted themselves as the South Kentucky Association in 1787. Associationalism was firmly entrenched among both Regular and Separate Baptists before the end of the decade.[17]

Across the Ohio, Baptists from Connecticut, New York, and New Jersey floated down the Ohio from Pittsburg and constituted the first Baptist church in Ohio on the Little Miami in 1790. Miami Association was formed in 1797 with four churches, all in the Cincinnati area. Meanwhile, "Mad Anthony" Wayne's victory over the Indians at Fallen Timbers in 1794 had opened Indiana for settlement. The Silver Creek Baptist Church was founded in 1798. The first Baptist services conducted by an ordained Baptist minister in Illinois were those of Elder James Smith who came from Kentucky to preach at Piggot's Fort in 1787 and again in 1790. Regular services were begun in the log house of James Lemen, and, in 1796, the New Design Church was organized. By 1807, several Baptist churches had developed in the area, and the Illinois Association was formed in January of that year. Two years later the Indiana work had also progressed to the extent that the Whitewater Association was constituted. Although there was a Baptist work in Mississippi near Natchez in about 1780, an effective witness developed more slowly in the Missouri, Mississippi, and Louisiana areas than elsewhere on the frontier. That was due primarily to a greater Roman Catholic influence. However, the Mississippi Baptist Association was formed in 1806, and Bethel Association organized a decade later in Missouri. There were three Baptist churches in Louisiana by 1813.[18]

The summary of it is that within three decades after the Revolution, the entire western frontier, from Canada to the Gulf of Mexico, felt the witness of Baptist churches and associations.

Sweet suggested that the greatest challenge facing the American churches, following the winning of national independence, was winning the ever-expanding west.[19] Those Separate and Regular Baptists, who soon set their differences aside to unite on the frontier, responded successfully to that challenge. By 1803, there were ten associations in Kentucky with 219 churches and 15,495 members.[20] Johnny Appleseed was warning of Indian raids, distributing tracts, and planting apple seeds in the Ohio Valley. Baptists were warning of eternal damnation, winning souls, and planting churches.

The minutes of Elkhorn Association included the announcement in 1804 of "the death of our aged and beloved Brother John Gano who departed this life August 9th aged nearly 80 years, he lived and died an ornament to Religion."[21] South of the Red River, Texas lay in limitless leagues from the Sabine to the Rocky Mountains. On the other side of the mountains, California, along with the gold-rich Oregon Territory, waited for the Baptist message. Others who were also "ornaments to Religion" would continue to have written after their names, "gone west."

Notes

1. A. D. Gillette (ed.), *Minutes of Philadelphia Baptist Association, 1707–1807,* for the year, 1781.

2. Walter Brownlow Posey, *The Baptist Church in the Lower Mississippi Valley, 1776–1845* (Lexington: University of Kentucky Press, 1957), p. 4.

3. Ray Allen Billington, *Westward Expansion—A History of the American Frontier* (New York: Macmillan Publishing Co., Inc., 1974), p. 157.

4. George Gordon Byron, *Don Juan,* canto 8, stanzas LXI–LXVII

5. Billington, p. 159.

6. William Lumpkin, *Baptist Foundations in the South* (Nashville: Broadman Press, 1961), p. 76.

7. William Warren Sweet, *Religion on the American Frontier: The Baptists, 1783–1830* (New York: Cooper Square Publishing, Inc., 1964), p. 27.

8. Ibid., p. 19.

9. Ibid., p. 22.

10. William H. Guthman, *March to Massacre: A History of the First Seven Years of the United States Army, 1784–1791* (New York: McGraw Hill Book Co., 1970), p. 84.

11. Gordon Carruth (ed.), *The Encyclopedia of American Facts & Dates* (New York: Thomas Y. Crowell Co., 1970), p. 48. The population statistics for 1720 were 474,388 and should have been approaching 600,000 by 1727 when John Gano was born.

12. David Benedict, *A General History of the Baptist Denomination in America and Other Parts of the World* (New York: Lewis Colby and Co., 1848), pp. 364–65.

13. Carruth, *Facts & Dates,* reports the population in 1800 to have been 5,308,483 (p. 118) and as 7,239,881 in 1810 (p. 132). In 1804, the population should have been about 6,000,000. And Benedict (p. 366), reported that, in 1812, there were 2,633 churches, 204,185 members, and 111 associations.

14. *Encyclopedia of Southern Baptists,* "Gano, John," and *Dictionary of American Biography,* "Gano, John," and John Gano, *Biographical Memoirs of the Late Rev. John Gano of Frankfort* (New York: Southwicke and Hardcastle, 1806).

15. Sweet, p. 22.

16. Posey, selected from pp. 19–33.

17. Sweet, pp. 22–23.

18. Ibid., pp. 28–35.

19. Ibid., p. 18.

20. Ibid., p. 25.

21. Ibid., p. 504.

3.

THE ASSOCIATION AND THE FINAL SURGE OF BAPTISTS TO THE PACIFIC

They crawled up the slopes, and the low twisted trees covered the slopes. Holbrook, Joseph City, Winslow. And then the tall trees began, and the cars spouted steam and labored up the slopes. And there was Flagstaff, and that was the top of it all. Down from Flagstaff over the great plateaus, and the road disappeared in the distance ahead. The water grew scarce. . . . The sun drained the dry rocky country, and ahead were the jagged peaks, the western wall of Arizona . . . . They drove all night . . . and when the daylight came they saw the Colorado River below them.

Pa called, "We're there—we're in California!"

John Steinbeck
The Grapes of Wrath

US Highway 281 unrolls in a long undulating ribbon northward from San Antonio across sprawling Central Texas hills. Hidden in a cedar thicket beside the highway ten miles north of Lampasas is a forgotten cemetery. Overgrown, reclaimed by deer and armadillos, its decaying and discolored markers are shrouded in mystery. Miller, Stanley, Holley, Willis—those were the families. They were Allies, Johns, Ediths, Rachels—names that were typical of their times.

Some of them lived amazingly long lives, more than double their century's expected life span. There is the marker of John Stanley, born in 1806, but not planted in the Texas sod until eighty-eight years later. His wife, Edith, was born in 1804, the year John Gano was mourned by Kentucky's Elkhorn Association. She died in 1889.

Perhaps the most provocative marker is that of Rachel Willis. Appropriately named in her century, Rachel was born only nine years after the Revolution. She lived until a dozen years after the Civil War. One wonders where Rachel came from and why she wound up in a Central Texas grave. What route brought her to that place? Where were the stops along the way?

Rachel was not born there. Millers, Stanleys, Holleys, Willises were not found anywhere in Texas when the nineteenth century began, nor in significant numbers before its third decade. They were found in the heart of the country's beginnings. Those, and others like them, are the names recorded in the eighteenth-century minutes of Philadelphia Association, and in the Charleston and Virginia associations. By 1792, when Rachel Willis first filled her tiny lungs, they were beginning to abound in Kentucky and Tennessee, which was the western frontier when the eighteenth century expired.

By the 1820s, the frontier was moving on, always farther west. Most of the first Texas settlers moved there from states that are located in the Mississippi Valley. Rachel, and the others of that cemetery's forgotten ones, probably did too. Likely, they, or their parents before them, had followed Boone's Wilderness Road to the Kentucky-Tennessee frontier, or, like Gano, had floated down the Ohio. Ever pioneers, as the frontier moved on to Texas, they moved with it. That was the frequent script.

Stephen F. Austin, who planted the first Anglo-American colony in Texas in 1822, arrived there by way of Virginia, Missouri, and Arkansas. Colonel James Walker Fannin, who was shot at Santa Anna's command at Goliad, came from Georgia. William B. Travis, who commanded the unlucky

"Texicans" at the Alamo, got there by way of Alabama.

But more of the early Texas settlers came from Tennessee than from anywhere else. Young giants from the universities of Tennessee and Texas used to tilt back and forth across the Cotton Bowl on some January firsts. All dressed in orange and white, it looked like a family fight. Certainly many of them were from the same stock. Davy Crockett was one who barely made it from Tennessee to Texas in time to die in the Alamo in February of 1836. Sam Houston, one year younger than Rachel Willis, was born in Virginia but moved to Tennessee in 1807 and on to Indian Territory in 1829. By 1833, he had made it to Nacogdoches, Texas.

The best remembered Baptist of those early Texas pioneers was Zacharius N. Morrell. He arrived from Tennessee in 1835 and also stopped at Nacogdoches where he preached from Isaiah 35:1. His was not the first Baptist sermon in Texas. Freeman Smalley was at Pecan Point on the Red River in 1822 and may have had the distinction of preaching the first Baptist sermon in Texas in the home of William Newman. Joseph Bays, who was born in North Carolina but moved as a boy to Kentucky, preached the first sermon west of the Brazos in the home of Moses Shipman in 1823. In 1829, Thomas Hanks was preaching near San Felipe, also in the home of Shipman. In the same year, Thomas J. Pilgrim, from New York, started a Sunday School in a log room at San Felipe. Another Sunday School was begun at the same time in the home of William Kincheloe at El Caney near Wharton. In 1834, Isaac Reed, another who made the move from Tennessee, was preaching in East Texas.

But while others preceded him on the scene, it was Morrell who led in organizing what is acknowledged to have been the first "regular missionary Baptist church" in Texas at Washington in 1837. Jesse Mercer, president of the Triennial Convention, endorsed that church's request that Texas be considered a mission field, and James Huckins landed in Galveston in January 1840, as the first Baptist missionary to Texas. Thousands of people were pouring through that port into the Republic of Texas in that decade. Huckins had soon organized churches in both Galveston and Houston.

As always, associationalism soon followed the founding of churches. The same year, 1840, saw the birth of Union Association. That event turned out to be a momentous one to Baptists of America. Within another year, missionary William Tryon, who recently had joined Huckins, had encouraged Union Association to form an education society, from which Baylor University developed in 1845. The Texas Baptist Home Mission Society was also formed in 1841. Three missionaries were appointed, one of whom was Morrell.[1]

Texas proved to be a fruitful field for Baptists. By 1848, the denomination had grown sufficiently in the state to be listed in Benedict's history. He reported four associations with a total membership of 1,388.[2] That year also saw messengers from those four associations and thirty-five churches meet at Anderson to organize the Baptist State Convention of Texas. By 1853, there were eleven associations in Texas. The high priority given to the Texas work by the Domestic Mission Board of the Southern Baptist Convention is reflected in Arthur B. Rutledge's statement that by 1860, "thirty-three missionaries had been sent to Texas."[3]

Rutledge also noted that "work had started well on the west coast" by 1860. Conestoga wagons, the nineteenth-century's self-contained mobile homes, in long lines one behind the other, lurched across the plains and through the passes into California and Oregon.

Baptist preachers arrived shortly after the first rush. Osgood Church Wheeler, under appointment of the American Baptist Home Mission Society, organized the first Baptist church in California at San Francisco on July 6, 1849.

Churches were organized at San Jose and in Sacramento City in 1850. Again, associationalism followed almost immediately. Those first three churches formed the San Francisco Baptist Association in 1851, which solicited correspondence with the American Baptist Home Mission Society, the Southern Baptist Convention, the American Baptist Publication Society, and the American Indian Mission Association. Other churches continued to be born. First Baptist of Santa Clara was formed in 1851, Santa Rosa in 1852, and El Monte in 1853. For thirteen years, the El Monte church was the only Baptist church in Southern California. Most of its members came from Texas, Arkansas, and Missouri.[4]

Two who served significantly in California were Jehu Lewis Shuck and E. J. Willis. Shuck, who formerly had been a missionary to China for the Triennial Convention, and still later for the Southern Baptist Convention, was appointed by the Domestic Mission Board in 1854. He served for a time as pastor of the Sacramento church where his labors were rewarded with successes among both the Chinese and white settlers. E. J. Willis, an attorney from Virginia, in whose home the Sacramento church had been organized, was the first County Judge of Sacramento, having been elected to that position in 1850. The judge quit judging, went to preaching, and organized the First Baptist Church of Oakland in 1854, at which time he was appointed to missionary service by the Domestic Mission Board. Sam Harvey noted that "much of the credit of the support of the California Mission must be given to Goshen Association in Virginia. It was this association that gave $850 so that Shuck might go to California." By 1860, there were fifty-three Baptist churches in California, three associations, and 1,825 members.[5]

The Civil War caused the termination of the nineteenth-century phase of Southern Baptists' witness in California.

The American Baptist Home Mission Society continued a worthy ministry for Baptists in California after the Southern Baptist withdrawal. That ministry was facilitated by the fact that all of the Baptist churches, whether of Southern Baptist or American Baptist Home Mission Society origin, had affiliated with the same associations. Baptist successes subsequent to the war were reflected in the minutes of their annual meetings. The committee on Home Missions of Los Angeles Association, whose churches were affiliated with the California State Convention, called attention late in the nineteenth century to "the great work of the American Baptist Home Mission Society whose motto fitly expresses its great field of labor." That motto was "North America for Christ." The committee reported: "Especially in our own state in the planting of new churches . . . has the Home Mission Society done us invaluable service, returning to us manyfold the money paid into their treasury." When that was written in the last decade of the nineteenth century, the association was composed of thirty-eight churches with more than 3,600 members from Los Angeles, San Diego, San Bernardino, Riverside, San Jacinto, and Redlands. At the same time, it was anticipating the start of new ministries in Paso Robles, Oceanside, Escondido, Poway, Ramona, Julian, Banning, Beaumont, and Ontario. Los Angeles Association, while planning those extensive outreach efforts, evidenced the same healthy desire to reach Orientals that continues to characterize Baptist efforts in that sprawling metropolitan giant. The association declared:

Nowhere can the saving power of the gospel be so successfully and economically brought to bear upon the Chinese as right here. . . . Therefore, Resolved, that we urgently recommend that every church establish, and earnestly and patiently prosecute a Gospel Mission School among the Chinese whom God has brought within their reach.[6]

In the first decade of the twentieth century, the San Joaquin Valley Association, which was also affiliated with the California Baptist State Convention, reported that several fields had received missionary attention the past year. The ethnic nature of California work again was emphasized in the report that a new Danish church had been organized at Selma.[7] The same association declared in 1928 that "State missions are fundamental to all other missions" and reported that thirty-four missionaries and sixteen teachers in the Chinese schools were being supported jointly by the State Convention and the Home Mission Society. But the same annual meeting of San Joaquin Valley Association deplored the fact that, in 1928, in San Francisco, "that great city with a population of over 400,000, we have only 1420 Baptists." The report concluded, "The East is pouring its 60,000 to 100,000 a year into California, and some thousands or so are Baptists." The question, which is still pertinent today, then was asked of the association's Baptist people: "Shall we keep up our Baptist churches so as to enroll them in our work or let them drift to other denominations or lose interest because they do not find a Baptist church in the place they settle?"

American Baptists didn't know it in 1928, and wouldn't want it when it arrived, but help shortly would be on the way from out of the Southwest.

This time they came in Model T Fords that coughed and wheezed and stuttered and steamed and sometimes stopped. When they arrived in the 1930s to work in the lush cotton fields and orchards of the San Joaquin Valley, they, like their Pennsylvania forefathers two centuries before them, wanted a church "like the one back home." They wanted to sing "Standing on the Promises," "Higher Ground," and "The Haven of Rest." And those are the songs that Southern Baptists sang at the first meetings of their newly organized churches and associations. They still sing them today.

Southern Baptists had reached beyond Texas into New Mexico in 1912, when Baptists of that state affiliated with the convention, and on into Arizona in 1921, when the First Southern Baptist Church of Phoenix was organized with seventy-two members. But it was not until May 10, 1936, that Southern Baptists returned to California. First Southern Baptist Church of Shafter was constituted on that date with sixteen members, the same number that began the work in 1755 at Sandy Creek. Shafter bore another similarity to Sandy Creek. While eight of Sandy Creek's charter members were named Stearns, eight of Shafter's were named Mouser. In what was to describe Southern Baptists in California during their first two decades, every charter member had been a member of a Southern Baptist church elsewhere. Sam Wilcoxon, who influenced early Southern Baptist development in California, came from Arkansas in 1937 to serve as pastor of the Shafter church. By 1939, other churches had organized at Oildale and Lamont; and, on April 13 of that year, the San Joaquin Valley Missionary Baptist Association was founded in a meeting at Shafter.[8]

Following the formation of their first association, growth of California Southern Baptists was immediate and constant. Minutes of the annual meeting held with the Orthodox Missionary Baptist Church at Shafter in September 1940, reveal that fourteen churches sent messengers to the association. They sang "I Must Tell Jesus," "Higher Ground," "How Firm a Foundation," and extended "the right hand of fellowship to messengers from Sanger and Port Chicago."[9] The association had meant it when it declared that "the object of this association shall be to promote the spread of the Gospel within the bounds of this association." In the early years, those bounds were far-flung. The 1943 annual meeting met at Lamont, sang "The Unclouded Day," reported nineteen churches with 1,637 members, and, in demonstration of its extensive geographical outreach, defined the associational area as comprising "approximately 150 miles north and south and from the east line of the state west to the coast."[10] Southern Baptists still had a way to go on the Pacific Coast, but, like California quail, they were on the ground and running.

The 1977 Annual of the Southern Baptist General Convention of California reveals how well they have run. The record rivals the Sandy Creek saga. Those sixteen members at Shafter have multiplied in four decades to total 315,384 members in 954 churches and thirty-four associations.[11] There was a crash program, appropriately focused through the associations, during 1975 and 1976 to increase their total number of churches to "1,006 by '76." Although the goal was not attained, the emphasis gave impetus to missions outreach and laid the foundation for California Baptists' participation in Bold Mission Thrust.

Many of California's Southern Baptists, even most, still originate out of the South and Southwest. Almost every one of its twenty-five directors of missions do. However, that particular characteristic is changing. Certainly California Southern Baptists are not as "Old Country" oriented as they were two decades ago, when more than two thirds of Golden Gate Seminary's students came from the South, and three times as many were from Texas as from California. The churches regularly receive members from other traditions and backgrounds. The future may be written in terms of how successfully the old and the new meld; that is, in how well the tensions, which sometimes exist between those who grew up in a Southern Baptist tradition and those who did not, are resolved.

Further study of the 1977 state annual suggests that California is a microcosm of Southern Baptist work around the world. As would be expected, Spanish language churches abound. And scores more can be organized the first Sunday pastors who speak the language become available to lead them. But many other languages are also represented in the Southern Baptist witness to California: Chinese, Japanese, Korean, Slavic, Italian, Indonesian, Ukrainian—and in the Long Beach-Harbor Association, the only Samoan mission that exists in the United States. Also in Long Beach Harbor Association, but not only in that association, many black congregations are moving into the Southern Baptist Convention. The association has had a black moderator. The message is clear. Southern Baptists no longer are planting little patches of Dixie in California.

But while the work is complex and varied and while many congregations choose to maintain their ethnic heritage, there also is an admirable mixing that functions freely. The Central Baptist Church of Indio has had a pastor of German descent while the minister of music is of Mexican origin from the Rio Grande Valley of Texas. While Rene Garcia's life has been oriented more toward the Anglo culture in recent years, many of his friends with whom he worshiped in Texas attend the Spanish language services with *Primera Iglesia Bautista Del Valle de Coachella* only three miles from the Indio church. Some of the early churches in America's first association worshiped in the Welsh language because they had difficulty understanding English. More than two and a half centuries and almost 1,200 associations later and three thousand miles across the country, their spiritual descendants worship in a multiplicity of tongues.

The missionary outreach which began when Philadelphia Association broke out of its cocoon in 1752 is now firmly entrenched along the Pacific. That is true not only of California but also of Oregon and Washington—and of all points in between, as well as Alaska and Hawaii. Bold Mission Thrust is attempting to fill in the blank spots.

Perhaps the Baptist association's purposes will have been fulfilled when the objectives of Bold Mission Thrust have been attained, when every person in our land has had an opportunity to hear and accept the gospel of Jesus Christ and also to share in the witness and ministry of a New Testament fellowship of believers. But don't count on it! There will always be a reason for Baptist associations—until Jesus comes!

Notes

1. Robert A. Baker, *The Blossoming Desert* (Waco: Word Books, 1970), p. 12; Norman W. Cox, *Encyclopedia of Southern Baptists,* "Texas, Baptist General Convention of" (Nashville: Broadman Press, 1959); and Arthur B. Rutledge, *Mission to America* (Nashville: Broadman Press, 1969), p. 26.

2. David Benedict, *A General History of the Baptist Denomination in America and Other Parts of the World* (New York: Lewis Colby and Co., 1848), p. 954.

3. Rutledge, p. 26.

4. Sam Harvey, *The Southern Baptist Contribution to the Baptist Cause in California Prior to 1890* (Unpublished Master's Thesis, Golden Gate Seminary, 1958), pp. 1–4; and *Encyclopedia of Southern Baptists,* "California, Southern Baptist General Convention of."

5. Harvey, pp. 4–21.

6. Los Angeles Association Minutes, 1890 (not SBC).

7. Minutes of San Joaquin Valley Association, 1905 (not SBC).

8. *Encyclopedia of Southern Baptists,* "California, Southern Baptist General Convention of."

9. Minutes of San Joaquin Valley Missionary Baptist Association, 1940 (SBC).

10. Ibid., 1943.

11. *Annual of The Southern Baptist General Convention of California, 1977,* p. 238.

PART II
THE ASSOCIATION'S INWARD ADVANCE INTO THE LIFE OF AMERICA

We come now to speak of an association, by which we mean no more than a number of churches in sister relation, mutually agreeing to meet by their delegates, at stated seasons, for free conferences, on those matters that concern the general good of the churches.

Circular Letter
Shaftsbury Association, 1791

From before the Revolutionary War, and well into the nineteenth century, the most important Baptist event of the year was the annual meeting of the association. It met in the fall and sometimes lasted for several days. Philadelphia Association convened, usually at 3:00 P.M., on a Tuesday in October and adjourned the following Thursday morning. Charleston Association met in November. Warren Association, in its early years, had its annual meeting on a Tuesday and Wednesday in September. Some associations continued through the weekend. Some met twice annually at different locations. Virginia's Roanoke Association, which for a time did that, gathered in May 1812, at the Brick Creek Meeting House and again in October at the White Thorn Meeting House.

When the association met, Baptists were refreshed and refueled for another year. James Clark, writing for the *Encyclopedia of Southern Baptists,* wrote that the "reports and messages fired the preachers and others present with a joy and enthusiasm that enabled them to return to their work with a renewed energy and zeal." Not only were those who attended the annual meeting "fired" but so were many people who lived along the route traveled to the association by the preachers. Sometimes that was a distance of several hundred miles. Often several preaching stops were scheduled.

What happened when the association met did more than revive Baptists. It gave shape to Baptist history. At the annual meeting, the association blazed the trail for the denomination. Organizational structure, doctrine, polity—all were largely determined at the annual meetings of the associations. Actions that emanated from there shaped Baptist and sometimes national life. Many strategies which Baptists applied to gain religious freedom for all Americans, were developed in New England's Warren Association and in Virginia's General Association of Separate Baptists. The modern foreign missions movement was born at a Baptist associational meeting. It was there that outreach to the Indians was given great impetus in the first decade of the nineteenth century.

Two practices that developed in early associationalism were primarily responsible for defining the association's role in the denomination. One was the practice of receiving and answering queries at the annual meeting. The other was the practice of writing circular letters which were read and approved at the annual meeting and then circulated to the association's churches.

Queries from the churches to the association were being deliberated by English Particular Baptists at least as early as 1653. In that year, which was the fourth annual meeting of the South Wales churches of Ilston, Hay, Lantrissent, Carmarthen, and Abergavenney, one of the churches wanted to know "whether a deacon may lawfully mary after the death of his first wief."[1] The association agreed that it was lawful to do so. Philadelphia Association was responding to queries by the early 1720s. In 1724, the minutes of the association related that it was agreed, in response to a query, that a believer who married an unbeliever should be censured. Baptists are a consensus people. By answering the queries that were submitted from the churches, Baptist associations established the consensus which continues to condition denominational life today.

Circular letters, although they were not called that at first, were written to the churches almost from the beginning of associationalism. Particular Baptists' Midlands Association addressed a letter, which was circular in nature, "to the severall churches of Jesus Christ" from the "messengers of the severall Congregations met together at Goucester the 13thly of the 8th month 1657."[2] England's General Baptists were calling theirs a circular letter by 1692. Minutes of their General Assembly of that year included this:

The assembly taking into the consideracons the Messengers (itin- erant missionaries) sent to preach the Gospell in the several parts of the Kingdome have ordered Circular Letters to be sent to all the Churches of the same faith and order with us to Exort them to give assistance by an yearly Contribucon.[3]

The 1729 minutes of Philadelphia Association reveal that a circular letter, although it was not called that, was ad- dressed to "Dear beloved Brethren in the Lord Jesus Christ." Such letters, called the Pastoral Address, were in- cluded as a part of the minutes until 1767 when the name was changed to circular letter. In 1774, the association adopted a plan of dealing with one of its articles of faith each year in the circular letter. How that would influence Baptist life in America could have been forecast from the first letter which was written by Abel Morgan on the first article of faith. Writing about the Holy Scriptures, Morgan began: "These writings are of God, divinely inspired; the Word of God, the mind of Christ; of Divine authority; the infallible ground of faith and certain rule of obedience."[4]

The significance of the annual meetings can hardly be exaggerated. Through the circular letters and the associa- tion's answers to queries, Baptist doctrine and practice took shape. There at the annual meeting, through the wide ac- ceptance that it earned for itself, the association became an enabling agent which assisted Baptists, not only to ad- vance across the land geographically but also to make in- ward advances into the heart and fabric of both denomina- tional and national existence. Its influence has been more far-reaching and extensive than even Baptists have un- derstood.

Chapter 4 will deal with the association's developing defi- nition as well as with seven miscellaneous areas in Baptist life that were influenced by associationalism. The following chapters will then discuss four other areas in which the association brought major influence to bear.

Notes

1. B. R. White (ed.), *Association Records of the Particular Baptists of England, Wales, and Ireland to 1660* (London: The Baptist Historical Society, 1971), South Wales Association, p. 7.

2. Ibid., Midlands Association, pp. 35–36.

3. W. T. Whitley (ed.), *Minutes of the General Baptist Churches in England, 1654–1728* (London: Kingsgate Press, 1909), p. 38.

4. A. D. Gillette (ed.), *Minutes of Philadelphia Baptist Association, 1707–1807* (Microfilm, Historical Commission, SBC), p. 137.

4.
THE ASSOCIATION'S DEVELOPING DEFINITION AND MISCELLANEOUS INFLUENCES

Although the particular Congregations be distinct and severall Bodies, every one a compact and knit Citie in it selfe; yet are they all to walk by one and the same Rule, and by all means convenient to have counsell and help one of another in all needful affaires of the Church, as members of one body in the common faith under Christ, their onely head."

The London Confession of 1644

The founding principle upon which Baptists made their entry into world history as a recognizable religious entity was the principle of soul freedom. Baptism by immersion was not first. Spiritual autonomy for the individual soul— that was first. Consequently, it was inevitable that the concept of autonomy would be integrally involved in associationalism's developing definition.

The concept of soul freedom was voiced dramatically, but with tragic results, by the pastor of the first Baptist (General) church founded on English soil. Thomas Helwys wrote a book entitled *A Short Declaration of the Mistery of Iniquity* which was published in 1612. He presented a copy of the book to King James I in which he had inscribed the following: "The King is mortall man and not God, therefore hath no power over ye immortall souls of his subjects to make laws and ordinances for them, and to set spiritual lords over them." Helwys was cast into Newgate Prison and was not heard from again until his death a few years later.

But his concept of soul freedom was heard from again. Half a century later, General Baptists sent a copy of The Standard Confession of 1660 to King James's grandson, Charles II. It also demanded freedom for the individual soul. Article XXIV said:

That it is the will and mind of God (in these Gospel times) that all men should have the free liberty of their own consciences in matters of Religion, or Worship, without the least oppression or persecution, as simply upon that account; and for any in Authority otherwise to act, we confidently believe is expressly contrary to the mind of Christ.[1]

Autonomy for the Local Church

Local church autonomy is a logical extension of individual autonomy. It is a position that Baptists took early in their history. Also arrived at early and perpetuated throughout Baptist history is the fact that associations, with a few lamentable exceptions, have been protectors of local church autonomy. Walter Shurden declared: "Extensive reading in associational documents is not required for one to be convinced that Baptists were more interested in the freedom of the local church than they were in extending the power of the associated body."[2] Hugh Wamble pointed out that the first rule of the General Assembly of 1689 said:

We disclaim all manner of superiority and superintendency over the churches, and that we have no authority or power to prescribe or impose anything upon the faith or practice of any of the churches of Christ. Our whole intendment is to be helpers together of one another by way of counsel and advice.[3]

Benjamin Griffith, in an essay on the Baptist association which was published in the form of a circular letter in the 1749 annual minutes of Philadelphia Association, wrote:

74

"That an association is not a superior judicature, having superior power over the churches concerned; but that each particular church hath a complete power and authority from Jesus Christ." In a similar vein, Georgia Association said it had "no power to lord it over God's Heritage . . . infringing upon the internal rights of the church."[4] New England's Shaftsbury Association said in 1804: "We wish to have it ever remembered that this association disclaims all pretensions to any jurisdiction over the churches that compose it; so that no resolution of the association . . . ought to be obligatory on them."[5] Many of the early associations made similar statements.

It should be noted, however, that as developing Baptist polity insisted upon autonomy for the individual and the local church, it, at the same time, also insisted that churches were morally required to associate with other churches. Just as the individual Christian was duty bound to associate with other Christians in a local church body, so was the local church to do the same with other churches.

Most historians have considered Particular Baptists' Abingdon Association to be the first Baptist association. It said at its organizational meeting in October, 1652:

That perticular churches of Christ ought to hold firme communion each with other in point of advice in doubtful matters and controversies . . . . Because there is the same relation betwixt the perticular churches each towards other as there is betwixt perticular members of one church.[6]

Eight years earlier, the seven churches who composed the London Confession of 1644 had said much the same thing. The Second London Confession of 1677 and 1689, which became the confession adopted by Philadelphia Association and, thus, came to exercise great influence on American Baptists, would say it again. "As each Church, and all the Members of it, are bound to pray continually, for the good and prosperity of all the churches of Christ, in all places; and upon all occasions . . . so the Churches . . . ought to hold communion amongst themselves for their peace, increase of love, and mutual edification."[7]

Autonomy for the Association

While the association has been a guardian of local church autonomy, it has been equally adamant in insisting that it, too, is an autonomous body. An association is a voluntary confederation of churches. Relevant to that, it should be noted that the traditional historical view has been that churches are the constituent members of associations, not messengers. As voluntary organizations, associations have insisted upon the right to determine their own membership, to exclude churches judged guilty of doctrinal heresy or polity disorder, and to regulate their own annual meetings. Shaftsbury Association affirmed in 1791: "In case any church, or churches shall apostatize from the faith, and become corrupt . . . it is the duty of this association . . . to inform the churches in general, that we consider those churches who have fallen no longer in our fellowship."[8] The minutes of Philadelphia Association, 1800, declared: "The association conceive that the regular business of the association is to take into consideration those matters which are introduced by the churches, yet, that the association consider themselves at liberty to take up any matter of consequence introduced by any individual member."

Definitions of Associationalism

Mutually autonomous—that's what all Baptists and all Baptist entities are. Associations have insisted on that. Most definitions that have been developed have reflected that concept. Russell Bennett formulated a very precise and inclusive definition in 1974 that was developed after studying much of the written material dealing with Baptist associations. "The Baptist association is an autonomous cooperative, usually in a given geographic area, voluntarily organized by autonomous Baptist churches of similar faith and practice, meeting regularly through equal messengers to accomplish purposes suitable to the related congregations."[9] The Inter-Agency Council of the Southern Baptist Convention declared: "A Baptist association is a self-determining Baptist interchurch community, created and sustained by the churches affiliated with her and responsible to them through their messengers, in which the churches foster their fellowship."[10] Meanwhile, an admirably brief and theologically simple but superbly practical definition is Loyd Corder's. He said, "The Baptist Association is free churches in fellowship on mission in their setting."

Miscellaneous Influences of the Association

Because the association had so satisfactorily established its place and so acceptably defined its relationship to the churches by the last decade of the eighteenth century, it was able to influence Baptist life across a wide-ranging spectrum. Through both the circular letter and the queries addressed to it, the association became the forum for discussion, and sometimes resolution, of those issues that confronted Baptists. They were sundry.

Discipline (including right order)

As has already been noted, a basic presumption held throughout the long history of associationalism is that the association has the right to determine who its constituents are. That has been considered a part of its rightful autonomy. That organizational principle necessarily requires that the association exercise some control over the doctrines and practices of the churches. For that reason, associations, almost without exception, have investigated churches who petitioned for membership to determine that they were established according to "right order and discipline." Benjamin Griffith, in his frequently quoted essay on the association which was published in 1749, said that "several such independent churches, where Providence gives them their situation convenient, may, and ought, for their mutual strength, counsel, and other valuable advantages, by their voluntary and free consent, to enter into an agreement and confederation." But he immediately added that, in those associated churches, "there must be agreeing in doctrine and practice."[11] In other words, the association should demand that all member churches be of "like faith and order."

Throughout most of associationalism's history, that policy of determining its own constituents has been extended to the exercise of a limited influence over the membership of the local churches. The Particular Baptist churches of Hay, Lanharan, and Ilston in Wales, a forerunner of the present-day association, said in November, 1650:

Upon further consideration of the subtilty and malice of the adversary in seekinge . . . to withdraw, if it were possible, the very elect from their stedfastness, it is therefore agreed . . . that the several churches be desired to take especiall care to stopp and quench all divideinge principles, that shalbe broached by or among, and of the brethen, and that shall or may in any wise tend to the subversione, or hinderinge of right order and discipline among them.

Clearly that association was urging its member churches to control the doctrinal beliefs and practices of their members. Three years later, when a group threatened to pull out of the Hay church, the association, which now consisted of six churches, ordered what was judged to be the divisive group to "forbeare . . . the receaving into or keeping in their fellowship, such as shall be cast out by the (recognized) church ministry, not practicing in their private meeting any such ordinances as are proper to the churches of Christ." This final warning was added: "And, in case they will not hearken to this advise, wee will at our next meeting, with one consent, declare against and disowne them."[12] More than a century and a half later, New England's Warren Association declared in its minutes of 1812, "That church which will not hearken to the counsel of their brethren, shall lose its place in this connection."

Usually the association has tried to bring reconciliation between the differing parties within the local church. That has been one of the historic values of associationalism. That principle was set out at the organizational meeting in Philadelphia Association in 1707. Records of that occasion which were kept by the Pennepek church included this:

It was also concluded, that if any difference shall happen between any member and the church he belongs unto, and they cannot agree, then the person so grieved may at the general meeting, appeal to the brethren of the several congregations, and with such as they shall nominate, to decide the difference; that the church and the person so grieved do fully acquiesce in their determination.[13]

That appeal to the brethren generally came in the form of a query, and the decision of the association was usually accepted by all concerned.

Education (primarily ministerial)

General Baptists, early in their development, gave priority to an educated ministry. But more significant to Baptists of America was the importance assigned to ministerial education by Philadelphia Association. As early as 1722, "It was proposed for the churches to make inquiry among themselves, if they have any young persons hopeful for the ministry, and inclinable for learning . . . to give notice of it to Mr. Abel Morgan . . . that he might recommend such to the Academy."[14] By 1761, the association had a library with two of the leading pastors in charge of it. By 1764, Philadelphia Association was pushing for the organization of a Baptist college. The result was that Rhode Island College (now Brown University) opened at Warren, Rhode Island, in 1770. Most of the financial support came from Philadelphia, Warren, and Charleston associations. Rhode Island College was named by William G. McLoughlin as being one of two institutions that gave "the Baptist movement in New England cohesion, status, and power."[15] The other was Warren Baptist Association.

From the standpoint of the Baptist future in America, the matter of ministerial education not only was significant, it also was controversial. Primitive Baptists challenged "the learned world to show any divine authority for sending a man to school after God has called him into the ministry."[16] A prevalent attitude among Hardshell Baptists, and others on the Kentucky-Tennessee frontier, was that a special spiritual wisdom was imparted with the call to preach which needed no refinement from human instrumentality. That same prejudice against an educated ministry also led to opposition to the developing Sunday School movement. It, too, was man's invention. Fortunately most Baptist associations successfully refuted such ideas. In 1791, Roanoke Association asked: "Can a parent bestow a more valuable treasure upon children than to give them an education?" The association answered: "If you wish to see your children useful and reputable, you must be thorough in their education."[17]

Perhaps W. W. Barnes packaged, in one paragraph, as accurate an evaluation as is to be found of the value the association has been to education. He wrote:

Out of the Education Fund (created by Charleston Association) chartered in 1791 came Furman University. The fund became the endowment of Furman and was the nucleus of the Southern Baptist Theological Seminary. It was given to the Seminary at its beginning in 1859. Jesse Mercer, educated by this Fund, founded Mercer University. Through his influence and gifts the first Baptist missionary went to Texas and began the work that led to Baylor University and out of which came the Southwestern Seminary.[18]

Officers

Article XXXVI of the London Confession of 1644 named the church officers of that day and clearly established that they were to be chosen by the local church with no coercion from any hierarchical source. "Every Church has power given them from Christ for their better wellbeing to choose to themselves meet persons into the office of Pastors, Teachers, Elders, Deacons, being qualified according to the Word . . . for the feeding, governing, serving, and building up his church, and that none other have power to impose them."[19] That early Baptist document established for all time to come the congregational polity that would determine how Baptists would choose their officers.

South Wales association's minutes of August, 1654, received a query "respecting the several duties of officers and private members" in the churches. In a long and ambiguous passage to present-day American readers, that early Particular Baptist Association discussed the church officers as follows:

Pastor.—"The greatest charge lay on the pastor," the association declared. His office was "to do all that tends to the feeding of the flock." He was to exhort, reprove, cast out, lead the sheep, watch, administer the ordinances of the church, give himself wholly to the Word and doctrine, and rule well, which consisted of "preserving purity of doctrine and discipline."

Teacher.—The early Baptists had a dual ministry, as did the Congregationalists. The teacher, in the context of their day, was one of the ministers of the church. "The teacher's particular office is to wait on teaching, to expound scriptures, and confute errors."

Ruling elder.—"Or helping office is, to oversee the lives

and manners of men, to whom also double honour is due. He also must take care of God's house." Early Congregationalists and Baptists had this officer in their churches. However, since there was always some doubt about the scriptural authority for the office, the time came when it was no longer filled.

Deacon.—"Who is to serve tables, that is, the Lord's Table, and the table of all others in the church, that shall want his service. He also is to be dedicated to the church's service, as the word deacon imports." Obviously the role of the deacon was not as significant in early Baptist life as it has become in modern times.[20]

The Particular Baptists of Philadelphia Association, as late as 1728, were still following the practices they had brought with them from Wales. In that year, the association responded to a question from the Hopewell Church, "What course to take in choosing a ruling elder in the church?" The clerk recorded: "We answer, that a church wanting ruling elders or deacons, as in other cases, should set a day apart, and by fasting and prayer, seek the guidance and direction of God, and then unanimously pitch upon one or more of their brethren to act upon trial in the office of ruling elder or deacon; and our judgment is that persons called upon trial in the said offices, may act by authority of the church, with as full power as if completely qualified; but not so teaching elders or ministers of the Word and ordinances."

Ordinances

Various of the old associational documents reveal the consensus reached on a number of subjects at the time of their recording. Three statements, which summarize the early Baptist position, can be made concerning each of the ordinances.

Baptism.—First, the Baptist concept of what constituted

baptism was clearly established by the London Confession of 1644. It declared: "Baptisme is an ordinance of the New Testament given by Christ, to be dispensed onely upon persons professing faith. . . . The way and manner of the dispensing of the ordinance the Scripture holds out to be dipping or plunging the whole body under water."[21] General Baptists agreed with that Particular Baptist doctrine by at least 1651. The other major Baptist movement in history, Separate Baptist, declared "that true believers are the only fit subjects of baptism, and that immersion is the only mode."[22] There has been virtually no disagreement among Baptists concerning the proper subject and mode since the mid-seventeenth century.

Second, some of the early Baptists practiced baptism as a Christian ordinance, not as a church ordinance. There has been less than unanimous agreement concerning the appropriateness of that! But there is no historical room to doubt its truth. Particular Baptists' Abingdon Association declared in 1653 that "When an administrator is sent forth by any church to preach and baptize, . . . that he be minded to exhort all such persons as he shall baptize to joyne themselves without delay to some church of Christ."[23] In other words, the convert was baptized first as a Christian and then urged to join a Baptist church. In the second decade of the eighteenth century, Abel Morgan, pastor of Philadelphia Association's Pennepek church, preached periodically in the house of John Evans at Montgomery. Several persons were baptized, but not into any church. The association documents leave no doubt about that. They were not baptized into Morgan's Pennepek church. Neither were they baptized into the Montgomery church since it did not exist at the time. They were baptized into Christ.[24] That practice was not unusual. Sometimes it occurred at the annual meeting. Walter Shurden wrote: "There were several instances . . . where a new or recent convert was baptized at an associational meeting without the request or permission of any local congregation."[25]

Third, early American associations sometimes accepted as valid the baptism by immersion administered by ministers of other denominations. In 1765, Philadelphia Association received a query from the Smith's Creek church asking "Whether it be proper to receive a person into communion who had been baptized by immersion by a minister of the Church of England?" The association answered: "Yes, if he had been baptized on a profession of faith and repentance."[26] Virginia's Dover Association similarly concluded in 1811 that it was not scriptural to rebaptize persons who had been immersed in "the Christian Church." In 1815, further deliberation resulted in a declaration "that when baptism is administered in a solemn manner in the name of the Father, Son, and Holy Ghost, to a believer, by immersion, it is essentially right, although there may be some circumstances in the administrator which may not be correct."[27]

The Lord's Supper.—Baptists have guarded the Lord's Supper more closely than they have baptism. Consequently, most early Baptists observed the Lord's Supper as a local church ordinance. With the discipline of members occupying a major portion of most church business meetings, it was recognized that only the local congregation could know whether a person's Christian walk permitted him to partake. Closed communion was the uniform practice of English General Baptists during their early history. There was one exception. The General Baptist messenger could administer the Lord's Supper in the "churches in generall." The messenger was an authoritarian figure in General Baptist structure, a denominational person who had authority in the local churches.

Particular Baptists, while generally observing the Supper as a local church ordinance in their early decades, were

84

never as strict as were General Baptists. Long before the American Revolution, they had become very lenient concerning the Lord's Supper. In what is a surprising illustration of that fact, Philadelphia Association declared in 1746 that "churches ought to unite in faith and practice, and to have and maintain communion together." The association was responding to a question about serving "transient communion to members of another church." The final conclusion of the association was that failure to do so was "inconsistent, and not to be continued in nor winked at."

The position of Baptists generally has been that the Lord's Supper was not to be administered to people who were not members of any church. The minutes of Philadelphia Association said that in 1786. Three decades later, Separate Baptists declared "that the church has no right to admit any but regular baptized members to communion at the Lord's table." One of the terms of union agreed to when Regular and Separate Baptists united on the frontier was "that believer's baptism by immersion is necessary to receiving the Lord's Supper."[28]

The position finally arrived at, primarily through deliberations at the annual meetings, was that the Lord's Supper was to be observed by those of "like faith and order." In recent times, that phrase sometimes has been difficult to define and apply. But there is little question but what Baptists have usually understood it to mean Baptists who are members, in good standing, of another Baptist church. While the influence of Landmarkism has pushed Southern Baptists toward a very strict interpretation of closed communion in some areas of the nation, Baptist history does not support a rigid position. In fact, it was not unusual for the Lord's Supper to be observed at the annual meetings of early Baptist associations. The minutes of 1729 reveal that Philadelphia Association, in planning its next year's program, intended to observe the Lord's Supper as a part of the annual meeting. Glynn Ford said that Virginia's Shiloh and Albemarle associations "often observed the Supper as a part of the annual meeting."[29] Walter Shurden affirmed: "During the period 1707 to 1814, the observance of the Lord's Supper was a regular feature of many associations, and not a rare, unbaptistic act occasioned by the loss of emphasis on local church autonomy." Shurden added: "Baptists certainly believed the Lord's Supper to be an ordinance of the church; but because they believed the church to be more than local churches, they were not timid in expressing the fellowship symbolized by the ordinance in Christian meetings other than local churches."[30]

Ordination

It was said, in 1656, of one who became a minister, "He spoilt an ingenious husbandman to become an ignorant preacher."[31] The equivalent of that is today's story of the young man who interpreted the sign in the sky to say, "Go preach," when it really said, "Go plow."

From early in Baptist history, associations have been involved in the ordination of local church candidates. The foremost reason for associational participation, recognized across the centuries, has been to avoid the unfortunate mistake of ordaining men who ought to be plowing rather than preaching. Associational records establish at least four principles as having guided Baptists in the matter of ordination.

1. Ordination was the business of the local church. There are exceptions to that rule. The Separate Baptists exercised exclusive control over ordination at the association level. However, it is also true that assumption by the association of too much control over the churches led to divisions among Separate Baptists. The principle generally applied by Baptists in America was the Particular Baptist concept that the local congregation had sole authority over the ordination of its officers. The basic document in early American

associationalism, which was the Second London Confession of 1677 and 1689, said: "The way appointed by Christ for the Calling of any person . . . unto the office of Bishop, or Elder, . . . is . . . by the common suffrage of the church itself."[32]

2. While ordination was a matter of local authority, the early churches invariably called on the other churches of the association to assist. That policy was followed in the eighteenth century to the extent that virtually no church would ordain if, for any reason, it was not possible to obtain assistance from other churches. Virginia's Strawberry Association said in 1822: "This association believes the right of ordination to be in the churches; nevertheless, for the sake of utmost harmony and fellowship among our Elders, . . . we believe it expedient for the churches to ask assistance of the association."[33]

Philadelphia Association had suggested in 1753 "that any brother called by any of our churches to exercise his gift, when approved at home, should before his ordination, visit other churches, and preach among them, and obtain from those churches concurring evidence of their approbation."[34] Along that same line, Charleston Association, in 1838, said: "We recommend to the churches composing our association, not to license any of their members to preach the gospel, until a trial of his preaching talents and qualifications for the ministry, of at least twelve months."[35] Such protective measures often prevented the churches from too hastily sending out men who should not have been ordained. It is at this point that the current practice, which is becoming widespread, of the local church ordaining without assistance of sister churches could lead to problems. Not only will more unqualified men be ordained but doctrinal deviations will result from less care being taken.

3. Men were encouraged, to the point of coercion, against launching out on their own without approval of the church

or denomination. In answer to whether "it was lawful for a church member to goe forth and preach to the world without the sending or approbation of the church," English Particular Baptists of the Midlands, in 1655, declared: "It is unanimously agreed uppon that it is not, except in extraordinary cases."[36] In connection with a later case, the association explained: "In such a disorderly going out, he cannot expect the prayers of the church for the Spirite of God to accompany him." The association then added this bit of coercive advice, "If any brother shall persist in such disorderly practice after admonition that it is the church's duty to deale with him as an offender."[37] That policy was being applied by Philadelphia Association in the mid-eighteenth century and by most associations well into the nineteenth.

4. Neither the association nor the church interpreted the participation of other churches in ordination as a loss of local autonomy. Perhaps that was because the principle usually applied was that the ordaining council's recommendation was not binding on the church. However, the church almost invariably accepted the consensus of the associated body.

What it adds up to is that the role of the association in the ordination of officers was a protective one. Especially was that true of those who stood behind the pulpit. In keeping with that protective role, it was not unusual for the association to circulate warnings against imposters. Philadelphia Association, in 1756, "Concluded to publish in a public print, a certain William Leaton, for his irregular proceedings, in going about under the name of a Baptist minister, when he neither is, nor ever was."[38] Shaftsbury Association, in its annual of 1815, similarly warned: "We would . . . warn our churches against the imposition of a man traveling under the profession of a minister of the gospel, of the Baptist denomination by the name of Joseph Smith. He is a person of middle stature, and size, dark complexion, black hair and eyes; a harsh and stammering voice . . . . When detected appears very passionate, has two wives, is traveling now in the Eastern States."[39] He was not the Joseph Smith of Mormon history.

The circular letter of Charleston Association discussed the person who was qualified for ordination in 1830. "How is the call of God to the ministry to be ascertained?" the letter asked rhetorically. First, the association concluded, a person who engages in the work of the ministry must be born of God. Second, he must possess a pure heart and clean hands. Third, there must be a desire for the work. Fourth, the person must possess suitable gifts. Fifth, Charleston Association's circular letter concluded, the candidate for the ministry must be able to prove his ability in the church.[40] Traditional among Baptists, relative to the call to preach, has been the idea that if a man has really been called of God, he will know it, others will discern it, and he will be able to do it. That was what Charleston Association was saying in 1830. One preacher who has struggled unhappily through three decades in the ministry related that throughout that time people have been trying to tell him he wasn't called to preach. That could mean his pursuit of the ministry "spoilt an ingenious husbandman."

Salary

From the standpoint of the frequently burdened pastoral family, no contribution of the association has been greater than the institution's role in raising the level of ministerial salaries. Soon after the Revolution, American associations were calling for a higher standard of living for pastors. Roanoke Association declared in 1790: "We believe that such as are called, qualified, and set apart to the work of the ministry ought to receive from the churches and congregations to whom they preach sufficient support for themselves and their families." That argument was expanded in 1793.

"It is ordained that they who preach the Gospel shall live by the Gospel, and if it be barbarous and inhuman to muzzle the ox in your employment, surely it is more so when you neglect to support the hands of your ministers. The frivolous arguments of poverty ought not to be mentioned."[41]

The circular letter of Shaftsbury Association dealt with "Ministerial Commission and Reward" in 1795 and, in essence, arrived at three conclusions. First, adequate support should be given to the pastor and his family. Second, the burden should be shared by all members of the congregation. Third, it did not matter what method of remuneration was settled upon so long as it was "not made by the force of human law."[42]

When salary was agreed upon, it often was paid in produce rather than cash. The minutes of South Elkhorn Baptist Church for 1798 include this: "We the subscribers do agree to give John Shackleford the different subscriptions against our name in property mentioned . . . as a compensation for his Servises." Those properties mentioned were 12½ pounds of salt, 12½ barrels of corn, 3 bushels of "flower," 100 pounds of "beaf," and, to the dismay of present-day Baptists, 36 gallons of whiskey.[43]

Despite action of the associations to offset it, prejudice against a paid ministry remained high throughout the early 1800s. Most pastors had to earn their living through secular pursuits, and many died in penury. John Mason Peck told of a Missouri pastor who was unusually successful "in the conversion of sinners and establishing churches." He served without financial assistance either from missionary societies or from the churches. With unusual acrimony, Peck asserted, "He died . . . early in September, 1824, leaving his land without title, and his wife and little ones without a shelter they could call their own."[44] The Baptist association can claim, accurately, to have reduced such tragic experiences.

Slavery

From the national standpoint, no issue was more major than slavery. That issue began to move toward the forefront as a moral and social evil with which America would have to deal shortly after the Revolution. Its poignancy was dramatically underlined in a query addressed to Elkhorn Association in 1786. One of the churches wanted to know, "Is it lawful for a slave being an orderly member and compelled to leave his wife and move with his master about five hundred miles, then to take another wife?"[45] Elkhorn Association adroitly sidestepped the issue in 1786. But three years later, Virginia's General Committee met it head-on when it adopted a resolution prepared by John Leland. "Resolved, that slavery is a violent deprivation of the rights of nature and inconsistent with a republican government and therefor recommend it to our brethren to make use of every legal means to extirpate this horrid evil from the land."[46]

Unfortunately for freedom of nineteenth-century blacks and for Baptist moral consistency, Eli Whitney invented the gin in 1793, cotton was crowned, and slavery was perpetuated. In 1796, Ketocton Association, which had joined in petitions to the Virginia Assembly in behalf of its own religious freedom, declared that slavery was "an improper subject of investigation in a Baptist association . . . and a proper subject of legislation."[47] In 1805, Elkhorn Association judged it "improper for ministers, churches, or associations to meddle with emancipation from slavery or any other political subject." Ironically, the same session that dismissed their black brothers' freedom as a proper subject of consideration saw the association deliberate a query from the Glens Creek church whether it was right for "Baptists to join in & assemble at barbacues on the 4th of July?" Displaying the too frequent proclivity of Baptists for turning from things that matter to things that don't, the association declared they should not![48]

Many Baptists did free their slaves. And some associations continued to oppose slavery. Virginia's Dover Association recorded in its 1817 minutes: "We . . . recommend to our Brethren to unite with the General Assembly for the gradual emancipation upon some rational and benevolent plan."[49] But with the passage of another four decades, affording forty more years of rationalization, Charleston Association could declare in 1860: "In reference to the present crisis, . . . we believe and profess that the institution of slavery, as existing among us, is sanctioned by the sacred scriptures."[50]

Notes

1. William L. Lumpkin, *Baptist Confessions of Faith* (Philadelphia: The Judson Press, 1959), pp. 232–33.

2. Walter B. Shurden, *Associationalism Among Baptists in America, 1707–1814* (Dissertation, New Orleans Seminary, 1967), p. 121.

3. G. Hugh Wamble, *The Concept and Practice of Christian Fellowship: The Connectional and Inter-Denominational Aspects Thereof, Among Seventeenth-Century English Baptists* (Dissertation, Southern Baptist Theological Seminary, 1955), p. 326

4. Emerson Proctor, *Georgia Baptists, Organization and Division: 1772–1840* (Thesis, Georgia Southern University, 1969), p. 58.

5. Stephen Wright, *History of Shaftsbury Association* (Troy: A. G. Johnson, 1853), p. 99.

6. B. R. White (ed.), *Association Records of the Particular Baptists of England, Wales, and Ireland to 1660* (London: The Baptist Historical Society, 1971), Abingdon Association, p. 126.

7. Lumpkin, pp. 288–89.

8. Wright, Shaftsbury Association, p. 34.

9. F. Russell Bennett, Jr., *The Fellowship of Kindred Minds* (Atlanta: Home Mission Board of the SBC, 1974), p. 87.

10. As quoted in ibid., p. 87.

11. Gillette, Philadelphia Association, pp. 60–63.

12. White, South Wales Association, pp. 6–7.

13. Gillette, Philadelphia Association, p. 25.

14. Ibid., p. 27.

15. William G. McLoughlin, *Isaac Backus and The American Pietistic Tradition* (Boston: Little, Brown and Co., 1967), p. 101.

16. Walter Brownlow Posey, *The Baptist Church in the Lower Mississippi Valley, 1776–1845* (Lexington: University of Kentucky Press, 1957), p. 21.

17. Garnett Ryland, *The Baptists of Virginia, 1699–1926* (Richmond: The Virginia Baptist Board of Missions and Education, 1955), p. 148.

18. William Wright Barnes, *The Southern Baptist Convention, A Study in the Development of Ecclesiology* (Seminary Hill: By the author, 1934), pp. 16–17.

19. Lumpkin, p. 166.

20. White, South Wales, p. 11.

21. Lumpkin, p. 167.

22. Ibid., p. 358.

23. White, Abingdon Association, p. 132.

24. Gillette, Philadelphia Association, p. 19.

25. Shurden, p. 94.

26. Gillette, Philadelphia Association, p. 95.

27. Ryland, p. 175.

28. Lumpkin, pp. 358, 359.

29. Glynn Roland Ford, *The Baptist District Associations of Virginia, 1766–1950: A Study in Baptist Ecclesiology* (Dissertation, Southern Baptist Theological Seminary, 1961), p. 148.

30. Shurden, p. 94.

31. White, South Wales Association, pp. 14–15.

32. Lumpkin, p. 287.

33. Ford, p. 159.

34. Gillette, Philadelphia Association, p. 70.

35. Minutes of Charleston Association, 1838.

36. White, Midlands Association, p. 23.

37. Ibid., p. 35.

38. Gillette, Philadelphia Association, p. 74.

39. Wright, Shaftsbury Association, pp. 144–45.

40. Minutes of Charleston Association, 1830.

41. Ryland, p. 149.

42. Wright, Shaftsbury Association, p. 48.

43. William Warren Sweet, *Religion on the American Frontier: The Baptists, 1783–1830* (New York: Cooper Square Publishing, Inc., 1964), p. 37.

44. Rufus Babcock, *Forty Years of Pioneer Life: Memoir of John Mason Peck* (Carbondale: Southern Illinois University Press, 1965), pp. 139–40.

45. Sweet, p. 421.
46. Ibid., p. 79.
47. Ryland, p. 154.
48. Sweet, p. 508.
49. Ryland, p. 154.
50. Minutes of Charleston Association, 1860.

5.

THE ASSOCIATION AND THE STRUGGLE
FOR RELIGIOUS FREEDOM

*It is a leading characteristic of the Baptists,
that, without Pope or King, for head—without
spiritual or civil courts, established by law—
without a Conclave of Bishops, or Convocations
of clergy—without legalized creeds, or formu-
laries of worship—without a ministry supported by law, or any human coercion in discipline, they are so far united in sentiment,
respecting the New Testament, that a free correspondence and communion circulates among
them. They have no king (on earth) yet they
go forth, all of them in bands—The Bible is
the only Confession of Faith, they dare adopt;
the final umpire they appeal unto.*

John Leland, 1793

Patriots were singing a new song on the eve of the Revolution. "The Liberty Song" called upon colonials to:

Come, join hand in hand, brave Americans all!
And rouse your bold hearts at fair liberty's call;
No tyrannous acts shall suppress your just claim,
Or stain with dishonor America's name.

In freedom we're born, and in freedom we'll live!
Our purses are ready, Steady, friend, steady;
Not as slaves, but as free men, our money we'll give.

Tories responded with a sarcastic play on words with a song
sung to the same tune as "The Liberty Song."

Come, shake your dull noddles, ye pumpkins, and bawl,
And own that you're mad at fair liberty's call;
No scandalous conduct can add to your shame,
Condemned to dishonor, inherit the fame.

In folly you're born, and in folly you'll live!
To madness ready, and stupidly steady;
Not as men but as monkeys, the tokens you give.

In answer to "Come, Shake Your Dull Noddles," Dr. Benjamin Church composed the "Massachusetts Liberty Song," which was published in Bickerstaff's Boston Almanack.

Come, swallow your bumpers, ye Tories and roar,
That sons of fair freedom are hampered once more;
But know that no cut-throats our spirits can tame,
Nor a host of oppressors shall smother the flame.

In freedom we're born and, like sons of the brave,
    We'll never surrender!
But swear to defend her, and scorn to survive
    If unable to save.[1]

The Struggle in New England

How Baptists related to the battle of the songs is not known. It is not likely that they sang the Tory songs, but how enthusiastically they joined in the patriot tunes also is doubtful. Religion was yet to be encompassed in "fair liberty's call." Certainly it was not as free men that Baptists were compelled to pay taxes in New England to support Congregational churches. The war possessed a dimension for Baptists and other dissenters that was not present for members of the "Standing Order" churches. Isaac Backus described that different dimension when he declared that Baptists "fought on two fronts," on the one "against the British troops for civil liberty" and on the other "against the patriot legislators for religious liberty."[2] The Baptist association was the battering ram on that second front.

Made subject to banishment in 1644, New England Baptists had precariously survived the seventeenth century as tiny bands of illegal dissenters. While the new charter of 1691 provided a toleration which permitted existence, it did not relieve Baptists of paying taxes to support Congregational pastors. A Massachusetts provincial law of 1692 stated: "The inhabitants of each town within this province shall take due care, from time to time, to be constantly provided of an able, learned and orthodox minister . . . and the whole town shall be obliged to pay towards his settlement."[3] Since those qualifications were seldom met to the satisfaction of New England authorities by other than Congregational ministers from either Harvard or Yale, that eliminated Baptists. An act of 1728 finally exempted Baptists from paying the parish tax, if certain conditions were fulfilled, but required them to obtain certificates from local assessors. Technicalities were often invoked by those officials to avoid granting the exemptions, and the result was that Baptists were still being jailed as history rushed toward the shot heard around the world.

That was the unhappy lot of Baptists when Warren Association was organized in 1767. Although officially tolerated, that toleration, itself, had become intolerable. Baptists were no more willing, in the eighteenth century's surge toward freedom, to share in the struggle against British oppression, only to be denied first-class citizenship in their own land, than blacks were to accept "separate but equal" status following their loyal participation in the wars of this century.

Warren Association became the focus of Baptist efforts to gain equality for dissenters in New England. A Grievance Committee was established to document inequities. There were many. The Ashfield case was the most widely publicized and, since it became the catalyst that concentrated Baptist protests, the most important. Ashfield, which was a village in the western hills of Massachusetts, was settled in 1751 by "New Light" Congregationalists. As sometimes happened at that time in New England, the congregation turned Baptist and had established a church by 1761. But "Old Light" Congregationalists moved in and called a Standing Order pastor in 1763. Under complicated and ambiguous terms of incorporation, the local assessor managed to prevent the Baptists from qualifying for exemption from the parish tax. When Baptists refused to pay, their lands were confiscated and sold at auction at a fraction of their value.[4] To justify their actions, Ashfield authorities contended that Baptists were not of a denomination worthy of toleration. They were described as being wild schismatics too "fluctuating and unstable to remain peacably within any respectable organization." Their so-called church was "a sink for some of the filth of Christianity in this part of the country."[5] With Warren Association pressing the appeal, the case finally went before the king, who ruled in favor of the Baptists.

Other less publicized persecutions occurred up to the eve of the Revolution. Isaac Backus related that three Baptists, "though they had given in certificates," were imprisoned January 26, 1773, at Concord, scene of patriot battle against the Redcoats only twenty-seven months later.[6] Only a few weeks after the tea was thrown into Boston Bay to protest an unfair tax, eighteen men "of the Baptist society in Warwick" were seized for the parish tax, hauled across frozen New England hills, and thrown into "Northhampton gaol" for exercising a similar right of protest.[7] Backus, in his capacity as agent for Warren Association, protested. On April 7, 1774, a Boston paper defended the right of Warwick assessors to tax Baptists in support of Congregational pastors. "We apprehend that every body politic have a right to choose their religion, and to enact laws for its support," the paper declared.[8] "Massachusetts Liberty Song" did not extend its worthy sentiments to religious dissenters.

Backus was commissioned by the association to expose such inequities and "to use his best endeavors . . . to obtain the establishment of equal religious liberty in the land."[9] He vigorously pursued that objective over a period of several years, at the same time remaining pastor of the church in Middleboro about thirty-five miles below Boston. In that pursuit of religious liberty, as Edwin M. Hearne's painting depicts, the association sent Backus to the First Continental Congress which convened at Philadelphia in Carpenters' Hall on September 5, 1774. He conveyed this communication to the Congress from Warren Association, signed by John Gano and Hezekiah Smith, two of America's most respected Baptists, both of whom would serve as chaplains to the patriot troops: "We conceive that we have an equal claim to charter rights with the rest of our fellow-subjects; and yet have long been denied the free and full enjoyments of those rights, as to the support of religious worship."[10]

A few hundred yards from Carpenters' Hall, in a meeting going on at the First Baptist Church, sixty-seven messengers to Philadelphia Association recognized "our much esteemed brother in the ministry, Isaac Backus," as a fraternal messenger from Warren Association and received an offering for "our brethren suffering under ecclesiastical oppression in New England." The association recommended further that the churches continue four days of fasting and prayer for the "interposition of Divine Providence in this day of public calamity."[11] That same evening of October 14, a Baptist Memorial was read to members of the Continental Congress which reminded them that:

The province of the Massachusett's Bay, being settled by persons who fled from civil and religious oppression, it would be natural to imagine them deeply impressed with the value of liberty, and nobly scorning a domination over conscience. But such was the complexion of the times, they fell from the unhappy state of being oppressed to the more deplorable and ignoble one of becoming oppressors."[12]

Persecuted, their protests falling on deaf ears, why did the loyalty of New England Baptists fall on the patriot side? Backus dealt with that question at the beginning of chapter seventeen of his history. He asked: "Since the Baptists have often been oppressed in this land, and would have suffered more than they did, had it not been for restraints from Great Britain, how come they join in a war against her?" His answer was threefold. First, Episcopalian persecution of Baptists in Virginia suggested matters would be worse with that church in ascendancy, which would have resulted from British victory. Second, an anticipated result of a successful revolution for the colonies was "a strong hope . . . of final deliverance to this land." Third, the recent revival which had brought many conversions to Baptist ranks "bespoke a design of final deliverance, and not of destruction or slavery."[13]

Any ambivalence about the war that existed among Baptists was removed by the momentous April events at Lexington and Concord. Benjamin Franklin wrote in obvious sarcasm of General Gage's Redcoats: "His troops made a most vigorous retreat, 20 miles in 3 hours, scarce to be paralleled in history. The feeble Americans, who pelted them all the way could scarcely keep up."[14] Backus echoed Franklin. "Hereupon the cowardly Americans drew the heroic Britons back to their ships the same day, with much terror and slaughter, although near 2,000 of their best troops were employed in the affair, which will transmit the remembrance of Lexington and the 19th of April, down to the latest posterity."[15]

Backus recalled that "those called minute-men gathered and marched off next morning." Middleboro had joined the war. The ensuing conflict was the common denominator that brought Baptists and the established churches together and projected Baptists into the mainstream of American religious life. However, there would continue to be one divergence in objectives. While members of the Standing Order churches struggled valiantly for political freedom, Baptists waged war simultaneously on two fronts. "While the defence of the civil rights of America appeared a matter of great importance, our religious liberties were by no means to be neglected," declared Backus. "The contest concerning each kept a pretty even pace throughout the war."[16]

The Virginia Front

Although the battle for religious freedom was engaged brilliantly in New England by Warren Association, the final victories were won through the petitionary activities of the Virginia associations. The struggle in the Old Dominion was against the officially sanctioned Anglican (Episcopal) Church. James Madison deplored the persecution of dissenters by that church when he noted that "the clergy can furnish their quota of imps for such business."[17] Baptists vigorously protested inequities practiced against them by firing frequent petitions at the Virginia Convention.

It was in March of 1775, three weeks before Lexington, that Patrick Henry made his famous speech to the Second Virginia Convention which was assembled at St. John's Church in Richmond. Later that same year, a joint meeting of the Northern and Southern District associations resolved to circulate throughout the state petitions to the Virginia Convention requesting "that the church establishment shall be abolished," and "religion left to stand upon its own merits." At the same time, they declared that they looked "upon ourselves as members of the same commonwealth, and, therefore, with respect to matters of Civil nature, embarked in the same common cause."[18] As in New England, Virginia

Baptists were combining the concepts of religious and political freedom. A year later, three months after the Declaration of Independence was signed, the General Association of Separate Baptists again presented petitions with 10,000 names. They declared: "Equal Liberty! . . . which though it be the birth right of every good member of the State, has been what your petitioners have been deprived of in that, by Taxation . . . property hath been wrested from them and given to those from whom they have received no equivalent."[19]

Unlike their New England brethren, who lost their aggressiveness once the conflict ended, Virginia Baptists slugged away throughout the war and continued to do so when it ceased. The religious establishment began to crumble before their relentless pressure. Baptists first won the right for their pastors to serve as chaplains to the troops. Then, in 1780, they won a limited right to perform marriages. A few years later, they successfully opposed the bill for a General Assessment for Religion. The landmark victory for Virginians came when the Virginia Statute of Religious Liberty was passed in 1786. It stipulated that:

No man shall be compelled to frequent or support any religious worship, place of ministry whatsoever, nor shall be enforced, restrained, molested, or burthened in his body or goods, nor shall otherwise suffer on account of his religious beliefs.[20]

However, the final victory for all Americans still had not been won. That came when the First Amendment to the Constitution became law.

While nothing should detract from the contributions made to the cause of religious freedom by various individuals, including John Leland, the accuracy of the Leland story has suffered from accretions across the years. The most serious of those springs from the supposed race between Leland and Madison for election to the Virginia Convention which was being assembled in 1788 to consider ratification of the new federal constitution. There even has been speculation that had he not withdrawn in favor of Madison, Leland would have won the election and might have gone on to occupy the high office James Madison later attained. Several facts suggest otherwise.

First, Leland was an eccentric who often rubbed even Baptists the wrong way, the kind of person who seldom is successful in politics. His concept of separation of church and state was more extreme than that of his Baptist contemporaries. He was against state-proclaimed days of fasting and prayer, against Blue Laws (or Sunday-closing laws), against the movement to abolish delivery of mail on Sunday, and against chaplains serving in the legislature. Like Roger Williams, he favored a total separation of church and state where religion received neither privilege nor pressure from the government. While many of his positions are supported by most Baptists today, they were considered extreme and radical by his contemporaries.[21]

Second, there is no evidence that Leland ever became a candidate for the Virginia Convention, in which case he could not have withdrawn in Madison's favor.

Third, he was a New Englander who was born at Grafton, Massachusetts, in 1754, and who died at Cheshire in the same Bay State in 1841. Seventy-one of his eighty-six years were lived in New England. It is unlikely that a Baptist interloper from Massachusetts could have won high political office in Virginia at that time against one as popular as was James Madison.[22]

Fourth, and most conclusively, Leland was an evangelist, not a politician. By 1793, he was back in Massachusetts, where thirty-eight additions were added to his Third Baptist Church of Cheshire to make a total membership of 163. In 1800, that banner year for Baptists, Leland baptized 214 converts, and the membership had grown to 394.[23] Typically a Separate Baptist, Leland's interest was in winning souls, not votes.

What can be substantiated is that Leland was a member of the General Committee, an agency constituted of delegates from the several Virginia Baptist associations for the specific purpose of gaining complete religious equality. In 1788, the General Committee considered the question "whether the new Federal Constitution . . . made sufficient provision for the enjoyments of religious liberty." The conclusion was that it did not, and Leland, in the General Committee's behalf, and at Madison's request, transmitted ten Baptist objections to Madison. Since Leland supported Madison's later candidacy to the Congress in 1789, it is logical to assume that Madison responded to Baptist objections by promising to amend the Constitution. In any event, Madison's efforts brought about the First Amendment. It contains what perhaps are the sixteen simplest, but most important, words written on the subject of religious freedom. "Congress shall make no law respecting an establishment of religion, or prohibiting the free exercise thereof . . . ."

It was much too big a thing to be credited to any individual. Thomas Jefferson, who is credited with being among the most important men in obtaining religious freedom, believed more was involved than his or any others' individual effort. He reflected on the past in 1808 in response to the (Baptist) General Committee of Correspondence. He wrote: "In reviewing the history of the times through which we have passed, no portion of it gives greater satisfaction . . . than that which presents the efforts of the friends of religious freedom, and the success with which they were crowned." He was even more emphatic in sharing the success in a letter to Ketocton Association, also written in 1808. "In our early struggles for liberty, religious liberty could not fail to become a primary object . . . and although your favor selected me as the organ of your petition to abolish religious domination of a privileged church, yet I was but one of many who befriended its object." Jefferson also wrote to Albemarle Buckmountain Baptist Church, "We have acted together from the origin to the end of a memorable Revolution, and we have contributed each in the line allotted to us."[24]

Notes

1. Lee Vinson (ed.), *The Early American Song Book* (Englewood Cliffs: A Rutledge Book, Prentice-Hall, Inc., 1974), pp. 20–25.

2. William G. McLoughlin (ed.), *Isaac Backus on Church, State and Calvinism—Pamphlets, 1754–1789* (Cambridge: Harvard University Press, 1968), p. 13.

3. William G. McLoughlin, *New England Dissent, 1630–1833: The Baptists and Separation of Church and State,* Vol. 1 (Cambridge: Harvard University Press, 1971), p. 113.

4. See McLoughlin, *New England Dissent,* Vol. 1, pp. 531–46 for a thorough discussion.

5. Bernard Bailyn, *The Ideological Origins of the American Revolution* (Cambridge: Harvard University Press, 1967), p. 265.

6. Isaac Backus, *A History of New England with Particular Reference to the Baptists,* Vol. 2, (microfilm copy at the University of California, Riverside), p. 272.

7. Ibid., p. 280.

8. Ibid., pp. 280–81.

9. Ibid., p. 276. Applied to Backus.

10. Alvah Hovey, *The Life and Times of the Rev. Isaac Backus* (Boston: Gould and Lincoln, 1858), p. 202.

11. A. D. Gillette (ed.), *Minutes of Philadelphia Association 1707–1807,* 1774.

12. As quoted in Hovey, p. 205.

13. Backus, Vol. 2, pp. 299–300.

14. As quoted by Rupert Furneaux, *The Pictorial History of the American Revolution* (Chicago: Doubleday & Company, Inc., 1973), p. 40.

15. Backus, vol. 2, p. 293.

16. William G. McLoughlin, *Isaac Backus and the American Pietistic Tradition* (Boston: Little, Brown and Co., 1967), pp. 133–35.

17. Merrill D. Peterson (ed.), *The Founding Fathers: James Madison, A Biography in His Own Words* (New York: Harper & Row, 1974), p. 29.

18. Garnett Ryland, *The Baptists of Virginia, 1699–1926* (Richmond: The Virginia Baptist Board of Missions and Education, 1955), pp. 95–97.

19. Ibid., p. 99.

20. Henry Steele Commager, *Documents of American History* (New York: Apple-Century-Crofts, 1963), pp. 125–26.

21. See McLoughlin, *New England Dissent,* Vol. 2, pp. 915–38 for a thorough discussion.

22. See Reuben Edward Alley, *A History of Baptists in Virginia* (Richmond: Virginia Baptist General Board, 1974), pp. 90–118 for a thorough discussion.

23. Stephen Wright, *History of Shaftsbury Association* (Troy: A. G. Johnson, 1853), p. 38, 64.

24. Ryland, p. 167–68.

ciations, was beginning to "break forth on the right hand and on the left" in its last decade. Two years after Carey lit the torch in England, the flame had leapt the Atlantic. Charleston Association was urging prayer for the "propagation and success of the Gospel among the Heathen."[2]

With the start of the nineteenth century, that new blaze of missions concern, which was kindled by Carey's venture to the Orient, can be traced in the minutes of the various associations as it continued to spread. Those minutes reveal that the concepts of national organization and both foreign and domestic missions developed concurrently. An example of that is found in the minutes of Philadelphia Association's annual meeting of 1799 where "a general Conference to be held every one, two, or three years" was suggested. By the next year, the call for a general conference was coupled with concern for missions outreach. The association received a query from the Philadelphia church addressed to the annual meeting of 1800 asking about the "propriety of forming a plan for establishing a missionary society." The minutes report that the association thought it advisable "to invite the general committee of Virginia and different associations on the continent to unite with us in laying a plan for employing missionaries among the nations of our continent." The emphasis was on domestic missions. One of the churches of Charleston Association was also asking in 1800: "Is there not, at this time, a Call in Providence for our churches to make the most serious exertions . . . to send the gospel among the heathen, or to such people who, though living in countries where the gospel revelation is known, do not enjoy a standing ministry, and the regular administration of divine ordinances among them?" The minutes record that the association agreed there was such a "Call in Providence," and then revealed its priorities at that time, relating to missions, by adding: "The particular call to us, seems to be to turn our first attention to that description of persons, mentioned in the latter part of the query." Like Philadelphia, Charleston Association's interests were with domestic missions. However, with the passage of another year, Philadelphia Association's circular letter of 1801 called attention to "the success of the brothers of our denomination in England" in their mission to "the idolatrous and far distant country of Hindostan."

So, as the new century began, the two mission impulses, foreign and domestic, were running side by side, accompanied by the call for a national body.

While Charleston and Philadelphia associations were sorting out their thoughts concerning both a national body and missions, Shaftsbury Association had the distinction of establishing an associational missions structure that could be copied later by a national body. The association's circular letter of 1802 detailed the plan for a board of missions which consisted of twelve members. There were six ministers and six others. The board's responsiblility was to raise funds and dispatch missionaries "to such settlements of the United States, or Canada, where the inhabitants are destitute of a preached gospel."[3] Within a year $78.94 had been raised, and Caleb Blood was sent on a ten-week preaching tour to the west from Cayuga Lake to the head of Lake Ontario. There is no indication that Shaftsbury Association considered its initial thrusts into Canada as anything other than domestic missions.

Warren Association, which had struggled so valiantly for religious freedom, also took up the missions cause. Its circular letter of 1808 rose to heights of eloquence.

When we contemplate the voluntary privations and almost incredible hardships of some of our missionaries, who have taken their lives as in their hands, and at every hazard have spread far and wide the fame of Jesus; when we consult the narrations of their perilous enterprises, and witness the astonishing success of their labours; do not our hearts burn within us to participate in their toils and in their honors?

Ever practical Shaftsbury Association, which influenced Baptist life out of all proportion to its size and location, nestled as it was in the interior of rural Vermont, went beyond eloquence. In 1810, minutes of the annual meeting informed its constituents that "were all the members . . . to pay six cents annually (to missions) it would amount to more than has been raised in any one year." Then, in 1813, with raised sights, members were challenged "to lay by the small sum of one cent a week for the missionary fund." This sentence leaps out from the minutes to seize one's attention and explain their suddenly enlarged vision. "The work of Foreign Missions began to be thought of in this body. The beloved Judson and his heroic wife had now been cast upon the American Baptists for support."[4]

That was the catalyst Baptists of America had been awaiting, an event that would add emotional involvement to the intellectual assent most denominational leaders already gave to missions. For, as Carey's commitment to India had sparked the missions movement among English Baptists, so did the conversion of three Congregational missionaries to Baptist beliefs fan the already prevalent and growing flames into a raging fire among America's Baptists. Their conversion is among the more remarkable events in American church history.

Adoniram and Ann Hasseltine Judson had sailed for India shortly after their marriage in February 1812, under appointment of the American Board of Commissioners for Foreign Missions, the country's first foreign mission board. Luther Rice, with the same Congregational credentials, had sailed separately toward the same destination. All three, from Bible study which began at sea but which was continued after their arrival in India, converted to Baptist views. The three new Baptists were baptized in Calcutta by English associates of William Carey.

That event became a significant turning point in Baptist missions. From that time forward, foreign missions would receive top priority. However, there were immediate problems presented by the Judsons' and Rice's change in denominations. They were left without a sponsoring board and, consequently, without financial support. As a result, the Judsons communicated with Baptists in America, and Rice returned home to make personal appeals for support. Although the British blockade was severely restricting American shipping in 1813, he arrived in September of that year. Rice went immediately to Boston where the Boston Baptist Foreign Mission Society had already been formed to support the Judsons. Two approaches followed after this meeting. First, it was "concluded to issue a circular, which should be sent to prominent individuals in different parts of the United States. This circular proposed a general cooperation of the churches."[5] Second, Luther Rice began an extensive tour, which was to be his lot for most of the rest of his life. The first stop was at the annual meeting of an association.

Minutes of the October 5 session of the 1813 association at Philadelphia tell the story. "Our brother, Luther Rice, a missionary lately from India, was affectionately invited to a seat with us." The next day he was asked to speak and "communicated very acceptable and pleasing information that numbers of heathen now hear the gospel and chaunt the Saviour's name." The enthusiasm of the reception accorded him is apparent from the minutes of the last day's session.

This association has heard with pleasure of the change of sentiment in Brother Rice and Brother Judson and wife, relative to the ordinance of Christian baptism and of their union with this denomination. As these worthy persons are still desirous of pursuing their missionary career, this association, feeling the obligations of the American Baptists to give them support, recommend the formation of a society of a similar kind with those already formed in New England, to be denominated The Philadelphia Baptist Society for Foreign Missions.

Five weeks later, Rice was before the Charleston Association on Monday, November 8, where, "Dr. Furman introduced the Rev. Luther Rice, as a member of the church at Serampore, India." The association clerk went on to explain: "He was accordingly invited to a seat, which he accepted, and delivered to the moderator a written address, on the subject of foreign missions . . . and was received with great affection." The association responded, not only with affection, but also by suggesting a plan to the churches for establishing foreign mission societies. Contributions were to be raised and channeled through the General Committee, which already was receiving funds designated to domestic missions and to education of young ministers.[6]

The experiences of Philadelphia and Charleston associations were frequently recurring ones. Association after association declared their support of the Judson's, often in affectionate terms. Baptists felt genuine emotional attachment to the young missionary couple on the other side of the earth. The movement gained momentum and spread so rapidly, with so many societies being formed, that within nine months of Rice's return from India, delegates gathered in May to found the Triennial Convention.

The significance of what had happened was: First, Baptists now had a national body; and, second, the foreign mission movement's future was assured. The conversion of three Congregational missionaries and the extensive travels of Luther Rice had brought the two together in Philadelphia, point of origin of so much Baptist history. Nothing of that significance would happen again in Baptist life until another

May, that one in 1845. The scene would be Augusta, Georgia.

Luther Rice did not lessen his personal dependence upon the associations. In a letter of September 1814, to the Judsons, in which he conveyed the good news of their promised support by the Triennial Convention, he added: "I have addressed a printed letter to the Baptist associations generally, and I am happy to learn that the subject is taken up by them with readiness."[7] From scanning only two pages of his memoirs, one can determine how extensive were his travels among the associations. Leaving Philadelphia on July 25, he rode horseback a distance of approximately three thousand miles to meet with associations, crossing back and forth to Virginia, North Carolina, Kentucky, Tennessee, and finally concluding that period of travel at Sandy Creek in October. He remarked that "fatigues too often overcome me, or perhaps I too easily yield to the inclination for rest." His mission board reached a different conclusion. They "reviewed with sincere satisfaction, the unwearied and successful exertions, during the year past, of Brother Rice, their agent." The board added that it could "scarcely conceive the possibility of his having occupied a sphere of greater usefulness."[8] In that three-month period he had met with thirteen associations.

The Baptist association is still at the heart of missions concern and promotion. More than one million people heard 2,266 mission speakers in 154 association-sponsored World Missions Conferences in 1977.[9] That is an annual experience in the Southern Baptist Convention. Baptist associations are endeavoring to convince Southern Baptists that, as Goshen Association's circular letter proclaimed in 1814: "The fairest opportunities now offer for a display of our zeal. Large fields are open before us . . . . The word of life is translated into many languages . . . . Let our substance be given up to honor the Lord."[10] As that same association resolved in 1818, "None of us are exempt: there is work for us all."[11]

Notes

1. David Benedict, *A General History of the Baptist Denomination in America and Other Parts of the World* (New York: Lewis Colby and Co., 1848), p. 366.

2. Leah Townsend, *South Carolina Baptists, 1670–1805* (Baltimore: Geneological Publishing Co., Inc., 1974), p. 118.

3. Stephen Wright, *History of Shaftsbury Baptist Association* (Troy: A. G. Johnson, 1853), pp. 87–88.

4. Ibid., p. 137. This was inserted in 1853 by the editor of the minutes.

5. James B. Taylor, *Memoir of Rev. Luther Rice* (Nashville: Broadman Press, Reprinted from 1841 edition, 1937), p. 129.

6. Minutes of Charleston Association, 1813.

7. Taylor, pp. 139–40.

8. Ibid., pp. 152–54.

9. As reported by the Department of Promotion, Home Mission Board in the 1979 World Missions Conferences Schedule, dated 6–1–78.

10. Garnett Ryland, *The Baptists of Virginia, 1699–1926* (Richmond: The Virginia Baptist Board of Missions and Education, 1955), p. 184.

11. Ibid., p. 195.

7.

THE ASSOCIATION AND THE FIRST AMERICANS

A few years ago all was darkness here; we knew not God, we were ignorant of the Savior. Our children, like our fathers, grew up in blindness of mind. Our sick had no hope, no comforter in their afflictions, and all was dark beyond the grave. Now, we are thankful for what God has done for us. We teach our children the ways of God, and many of them listen and attend. We visit our sick, we pray for them, and point them to Jesus Christ.

Letter from Indians to Triennial Convention, 1835

One writer called it a "Cherokee Tragedy."[1] It became "the trail where they cried" and where, throughout the cold, wet winter, they died.[2] Indians remember it today simply as "the trail of tears."

In 1834, the Congress created a special Indian Territory to accommodate the removal of the southeastern tribes to land west of the Mississippi. By 1835, President Andrew Jackson (Sharp Knife, the Indians called him) was acting to implement it. In his seventh Annual Message, he declared: "All preceding experiments for the improvement of the Indians have failed." Leaving little doubt whom he considered responsible for that failure, the president continued, "It seems to be an established fact that they can not live in contact with a civilized community and prosper."[3]

To help the Indians prosper and because they dallied about leaving their ancient homelands for others beyond the Mississippi, Jackson's successor, Martin Van Buren, sent soldiers commanded by General Winfield Scott to expedite the process of removal. "Old Fuss and Feathers," who was more compassionate than most of the generals the president could have chosen for the task, spoke to sixty of the chiefs late in the spring of 1838. "The emigration must be commenced in haste," General Scott informed the Indians. "The full moon of May is already on the wane, and before another shall have passed away, every Cherokee man, woman, and child must be in motion to join their brethren in the far west . . . . I come to carry out that determination."[4]

An observer described how that determination was carried out. "Squads of troops were sent to search out with rifle and bayonet every small cabin hidden away in the coves or by the sides of mountain streams to seize and bring in as prisoners all the occupants."[5] Possessions were lost, and in the suddenness of the action, some families were separated. The Cherokees were first herded into army stockades scattered across their nation, and later were transferred to one of four emigration depots on the Tennessee River to await their westward journey.

That journey from Georgia to Indian Territory entailed a difficult winter trek of 700 miles: first, northwestward across the center of Tennessee, through southwestern Kentucky and southern Illinois, then south to Arkansas, and, finally, due west to Fort Gibson. Many were old or else were very young. Days were grueling. Nights often were wet and cold. In the fierce winter of 1838–1839, the forest alternately shivered beneath icy fogs, or shook before frigid blasts that brought sleet and snow out of the northwest. Dysentery, diarrhea, pneumonia, tuberculosis, pellagra—all spelled death to four thousand Indians along the trail of tears. One-fourth of the Cherokee Nation perished between

Georgia and Indian Territory.

Several missionaries accompanied the Indians. Evan Jones, who had gone as a missionary teacher to the Cherokees at Hickory Log, Georgia in the 1820s was leader of one of the fourteen Cherokee companies that traveled the trail of tears. Jesse Bushyhead, a Cherokee native who had been converted in 1830 and appointed to missionary service by the Triennial Convention in 1833, led another company. The Valley Towns church moved as a congregation to Indian Territory. Its worship services and the missionaries brought some relief to the tragedy that surrounded them. During the journey, 170 Cherokees were converted and baptized.[6]

However, Indians would not forget what had been done to them. One missionary who accompanied the Indians said, "I felt I had been in the midst of death." A writer commented on the consequences of the trail of tears: "The shock of the round-up, the tedium of the detention camps, the miseries of the march to the west had generated a hatred so terrible it could hardly be contained."[7]

The Historical Backdrop

The Cherokee tragedy was not an isolated event in American history. Rather, such was the frequent backdrop, regardless of the century or scenery against which Baptist and other Christian missionaries sought to convert the Indians. Three hundred and fifty years were written into the trail of tears, just as a span of almost five centuries casts an influence over present efforts to minister to the First Americans. All efforts to win Indians must be viewed with an eye to history; for that's the way Indians view them. When that eye is properly focused, with all the prejudices tuned out, one begins to comprehend the failures of the past, as well as the difficulties of the present—and is amazed at the successes.

The history of North America suggests that the Indian

problem began when the first Europeans set foot in the Western Hemisphere. The dehumanizing process had begun centuries before Sharp Knife and Old Fuss and Feathers answered the particular cues history had for them. The policy practiced toward the Indians, when it was best, was patronizing. When it was worst, it degenerated to exploitation and extermination. John Smith bragged that "for a copper kettle and a few toys, as beads and hatchets, they will sell you the whole country."[8] John Winthrop, noting that many of the Indians had died of small pox, was pleased that God was making it possible for Englishmen to claim what he had promised them.[9] Such was the Englishman's "Manifest Destiny!" When missionary concerns were articulated, they too frequently were mere tokenism.

Not even missionary tokenism was involved in the commission given by Ferdinand and Isabella to Columbus in 1492. The kingdom that occupied their concern was temporal, not spiritual. "Our will is, that you, Christopher Columbus, after discovering and conquering the said Islands and Continent . . . ."[10] From the beginning, Spain's policy was one of conquest and exploitation. For more than a century, their galleons plied the waters of the Atlantic and Caribbean, filling Spain's treasury with America's gold. No mention was made to Columbus of evangelizing any inhabitants he might encounter in lands across the sea. Of the Tainos on San Salvador, Columbus reported: "They love their neighbors as themselves, and their discourse is ever sweet and gentle, and accompanied with a smile."[11] In striking contrast, the "Christian" nobleman who sailed for Spain responded to their hospitality by capturing ten of the "heathen" to exhibit as trophies of the exploration. Later, one of those "gentle" Tainos, having logically assimilated the message of that kind of Christianity, refused baptism on being burned at the stake. He was afraid other such Christians would be in heaven.[12]

Neither did the patent given in 1496 by Henry VII to John Cabot, the Genoese who was the first to sail to North America in England's behalf, mention conversion of the natives. He was commissioned to "subdue, occupy, and possess all such townes, cities, castles, and isles."[13] Again, the usual response of the Indians upon their first contact with Europeans was one of friendship. William Brandon pointed out that Casteñeda, in the sixteenth century, described the Indian people of the desert southwest who would become the feared Apaches of the nineteenth century as "a gentle people, not cruel, faithful in their friendships." And Cabeza de Vaca, who shipwrecked off Matagorda and made his way across Texas to Mexico in 1536, reported of the natives that he encountered, "Wherever I went I received fair treatment." The Virginia Indians of 1584 were characterized as being "most gentle, loving, faithful, void of guile and treason."[14] Thus one might plausibly argue that the "heathen" were less warlike than were their "Christian" invaders.

Although the charter granted by James I to the Virginia Company in 1606 spoke of "propagating of Christian Religion to such people as yet live in darkness," the first that reflected sincere intentions of the English to seriously attempt missionary endeavors was the charter granted by Charles I in 1629 to the Massachusetts Bay Company. It included the desire that the English "Maie wynn and incite the Natives of Country, to the Knowledge and Obedience of the Onlie true God and Savior of Mankinde, and the Christian Fayth, which is our Royall Intencon, and the Adventurers free profession, . . . the Principall Ende of this Plantacion."[15]

It was a laudable ambition. But several circumstances that characterized the early English presence in America permitted only a limited and ineffective pursuit of that missionary desire.

First, those adventurers had to struggle simply to survive. What energies remained after managing that, if they managed it, must be employed to show a profit back in England. Sir Ferdinando Gorges balanced the concern for Indian souls against the profit motive and candidly opted for the latter. "What can be more pleasing to a generous nature than to be exercised in doing publique good?" he asked. "And what more pious than advancing of Christian Religion amongst people, who have not known the excellency thereof, but seeing works of piety and publique good, are in this age rather commended by all, than acted by any; let us come a little near to what all harken unto and that forsooth is profit."[16]

Second, the early colonials brought with them fears and preconceived ideas which precluded effective missionary activities among the Indians. William Bradford wrote: "The place they had thoughts on was some of those vast and unpeopled countries of America, which are fruitful and fit for habitation, being devoid of all civil inhabitants, where there are only savage and brutish men which range up and down, little otherwise than wild beasts." He went on to speak of the possibility of surviving the voyage only to "yet be in continual danger of the savage people, who are cruel, barbarous and most treacherous, being most furious in their rage and mercilous where they overcome."[17] Such concepts did not precondition Englishmen toward evangelistic outreach, and it is not surprising that the first Pilgrim contact with Indians in America resulted in a battle.

Third, and perhaps this is most significant, the Puritan structure of society was not conducive to missionary outreach. The church and community were inseparable. One did not break away from the community to evangelize the Indian in his wilderness home. Rather, the community must first be established and secured with the church at its center, the country subdued, and the natives anglicized. Even the remarkable ministry of John Eliot, the "apostle to the Indians," was hindered by the Puritan concept of community. His approach was to resettle native converts in villages of "praying Indians" where they could learn the occupations and, ultimately, the culture of the English. That culture included the Puritan work ethic which was diametrically opposed to the American Indian's more relaxed approach to life.

It was King Philip's War that finally delineated how spiritually bankrupt colonial policy was toward the First Americans and how impotent efforts at evangelism had been. Metacom, cynically dubbed King Philip by the English, became the seventeenth-century's symbol of Puritan Christianity's failure. Metacom, who was the son of Massasoit, chief sachem of the Wampanoags who had befriended the English at Plymouth, rejected the Puritan God of wrath and led a last desperate attempt to secure his ever shrinking kingdom from colonial encroachments. The Wampanoags were destroyed in one of history's tragedies. King Philip was killed early one August morning in 1676, and, for the next twenty-five years, his head was displayed in true Philistine style on a pole by New England's victorious Christians. Surviving Wampanoags were sold into slavery for twelve bushels of corn or for one hundred pounds of wool each. Metacom's wife and son became slaves in Bermuda and were never heard from again. Like certain animals which are forced to endure captivity, the Wampanoags who survived as New England slaves did not reproduce well and had virtually vanished by the time of the American Revolution. In a final ignominy, even the memory of Metacom was so distorted that a guide, prepared by the British War Office for its soldiers a century after his death, declared: "Bristol is remarkable for King Philip of Spain having a palace nearby and being killed in it."[18]

The Baptist short-timer, Roger Williams, contributed

more significantly to bettering English-Indian relationships than did any other individual, with the possible exception of John Eliot. Perry Miller, a foremost modern historian, wrote of Williams that it was "in great part because of him the ultimate battle of extinction was staved off until King Philip's War."[19] His unique work with the cumbersome title, *A Key into the Language of America: or, an help to the Language of the Natives in that part of America called New England,* which was published seven years after Williams was banished from Massachusetts, revealed the depth of his compassion for the Indians. Few seventeenth-century Englishmen possessed the sociological outlook that would have enabled them to write the following poem which Williams included in the Key.

> God gives them sleep on ground, on straw
>   on sedgy mats or board:
> When English softest beds of down
>   Sometimes no sleep afford.
> I have known them leave their house and mat
>   To lodge a friend or stranger,
> When Jews and Christians oft have sent
>   Christ Jesus to the manger.[20]

According to Newman, there were two Indian Baptist churches in Massachusetts in 1694. But little of an effective nature was done until after the Revolution to reach the native Americans after the death of Williams in 1683 and of Eliot in 1690. There were occasional glimmers of hope. David Brainerd, the brilliant but rebellious Congregationalist, was one. After a brief ministry, he gave promise of a worthy work with the Indians. But Brainerd died in the home of Jonathan Edwards, to whose daughter he was engaged, almost as his missionary efforts began. Edwards, himself, although remembered for his contributions to the Great Awakening, accepted a call in 1751 to be a missionary to the Indians in Stockbridge. He organized a Congregational church which consisted of both English settlers and Indians. At about the same time, Daniel Marshall, who would become one of the prime movers of Sandy Creek Association's Separate Baptist movement, served briefly, along with his wife and three children, among the Mohawks of western New York. Marshall was a Congregationalist at the time.

With that background of hate and suspicion, and with those tenuous exceptions at outreach toward the Indians, serious efforts to reach the native inhabitants of America must await the birth of a new missionary enthusiasm.

First Associational Missions to the Indians

The new missionary enthusiasm and a new century arrived almost simultaneously—accompanied by a new feeling of responsibility toward the heathen. And it was the Baptist association that had the distinction of being the denominational agency to make the first missionary thrusts toward the Indians of the modern era. Shaftsbury Association led the way with Charleston Association close behind. Named for the first church founded in the area of Shaftsbury, Vermont, but also including churches in northern Massachusetts and New York, it would be defined today as being a small rural-urban association. The editor and compiler of the minutes of its annual meetings described it in 1853 as being "remote from the seats of Metropolitan Power." But across the years, Shaftsbury Association was blessed with outstanding leaders, and its influence on Baptist life has been extensive.

The move by that association that instituted serious efforts among the Indians came in 1801 with "a proposition . . . by Brother Covell, for raising a fund, by contributions, for the purpose of sending missionaries to preach the Gospel in distant parts of our frontier settlements . . . among the natives of the wilderness." The association voted to recommend Covell's plan to the churches with the suggestion

125

that they forward a "liberal" contribution to the next annual meeting.[21] At the next meeting, in 1802, the association took what turned out to be the significant step of establishing history's first associational board of missions to administer an associational outreach effort. The newly organized missions board dispatched Caleb Blood on a tour of several weeks duration to Upper Canada, that geographical area situated immediately north of Lake Erie and Lake Ontario. (Paradoxically, Lower Canada, to which the association also ministered, is above Upper Canada.) In 1803, the association trebled its outreach by sending Joseph Cornell, Lemuel Covell, and Obed Warren on tour. Stuart Ivison and Fred Rosser, authors of *The Baptists in Upper and Lower Canada,* reported that from 1802 through 1820 "the Shaftsbury Association sent no fewer than fifteen different preachers into this province on various tours which lasted anywhere from a few weeks to several months each."[22]

Their successes are easily charted from the minutes of the association's annual meetings. In 1803, it was recorded that Lemuel Covell and Obed Warren went among the Tuscaroras where "Elder Covel made them a talk,"[23] In 1805, Hezekiah Garton, after having been on tour the previous fall, reported that the Tuscaroras were favorably disposed to the missionaries, and this time it was the Indians who "sent a talk" to the association expressing both their thanks and "their earnest desire to be further instructed in the Gospel." The next year, Covell teamed with David Irish in a trip to the Tuscaroras, and the Indians included three strings of wampum with their "talk" to the association![24]

It was Covell's last tour. He died of typhus fever on October 19, 1806. But there was no waning of missions fervor. To the contrary, the circular letter of 1808 asked rhetorically: "Brethren, shall we wait and let them come to us? This, not more than one out of a hundred can do. The great commission says go to them. Let us, therefore, send them the news of a Savior . . . . In saving sinners of every tribe, he fills the earth with his glory."[25] Might-have-beens are the bane of history. But the Wampanoags might exist today as a people of New England had the seventeenth-century Puritans had that understanding of the Great Commission.

Eight hundred miles south of Shaftsbury, Charleston Association also heard the call to Indian missions—almost simultaneously with Shaftsbury's initial effort among the Tuscaroras. In the same year that Caleb Blood was first sent into Upper Canada, John Rooker was employed by Charleston Association to preach to the Catawba Indians. A school was established among the Catawbas, and a teacher was employed "to instruct the youth in the common branches of education, and the principles of Christianity." An important characteristic that would mark the work of Southern associations with the Indian tribes was observable in Charleston's outreach to the Catawbas. Native leaders were developed. Consequently, in 1806 Robert Mursh, who lived with the Catawbas but was of the Pamunkey tribe, preached to the annual meeting of Charleston Association "with acceptance to a large and affected audience."[26]

The practice of developing native leaders increased as Baptist missions to the Indians expanded during the first decades of the nineteenth century. The Triennial Convention took up the cause in 1817. Humphrey Posey was appointed a missionary to the Cherokees, and in 1818 he established the Valley Towns mission on the upper Hiwassee River in North Carolina. In 1821, Posey also established a mission at Tinsawatee, Georgia. Duncan O'Bryant and his wife came to the work in 1823. Shortly afterward, Evan Jones also arrived to serve as a missionary teacher to the Indian school, which soon moved to Hickory Log. The O'Bryants and Jones accompanied the Cherokees in their removal to Indian Territory. So did Jesse Bushyhead, a native Cherokee who had been converted to Christianity and who later became one of the most influential men in Indian Territory.[27]

Meanwhile, the Ocmulgee and Ebenezer associations of Georgia sent Lee Compere to Tucheebackee, Alabama, in 1822, where he established the Withington Mission on the Chattahoochee River. Compere's interpreter, John Davis, was converted and became a prominent Indian preacher in the Territory. Davis was the first missionary appointed by the Triennial Convention to serve among the Creeks after removal. Other natives who accompanied their people during the removal and who led in mission work in the Indian Territory were Sampson Burch, Robert Jones, and Peter Folsom. All had been students at Choctaw Academy in Kentucky.[28]

Developing Indian leaders is still the practice. Some of the most effective work ever done on the Navajo Reservation is being done in this present decade by David McKenzie, a virtually blind Navajo with a beautiful singing voice and an equally beautiful gospel story of salvation in Jesus. Many other examples of native leaders who are rendering effective service could be cited.

Baptist missionaries and their churches had given aid and comfort to the Indians during the ordeal of the trail of tears. Some churches moved as congregations from their eastern birthplaces to Indian Territory. Led by their missionaries and native preachers, they began to show growth in the decade following the removal. By 1843, Cherokee Baptists had organized an association. The Creeks had done the same by 1851.[29]

An event of significance to Indian missions occurred in 1842. That was when Isaac McCoy, who had gone to the Valley of the Wabash in 1817—but having failed to bring about an enlarged ministry of the Triennial Convention to the Indians—led in founding the American Indian Mission Association. Its avowed purpose was to promote the "spiritual and temporal interests of the aborigines."[30] With southern sympathy and support, that association carried on a useful ministry. Such stalwarts in Indian missions as Henry Frieland Buckner and Joseph Smedley served under its auspices. However, its work continually suffered from financial difficulties and, in 1854, was offered to Southern Baptists. The convention's Domestic Mission Board accepted the next year.

That was the boost Indian missions desperately needed. The newly named Domestic and Indian Mission Board was able to announce a revitalized and vigorous program of missions to three Indian nations in 1856. Buckner and ten native preachers were appointed to serve among the Creeks, with churches in Alabama, Georgia, and Kentucky providing the support of the native preachers. Joseph Smedley was appointed to the Choctaw Nation. Ten native preachers, most of whom were supported by associations in Alabama, also were appointed to work with the Choctaws. David Foreman, himself a native preacher, was appointed to serve with the Cherokees. His support came from Coosa Association in Georgia.[31]

While all work sponsored by the Domestic and Indian Mission Board suffered severely during and after the Civil War, Indian missions survived. The Cherokee Baptist Association was organized in 1871, and the Choctaw-Chickasaw Baptist Association, oldest association in Oklahoma holding continuous sessions, was organized in 1872.[32] The declaration was made by the Home Mission Board in 1882 that "The Indian Mission . . . merits and will receive at our hands great consideration . . . and increased expenditures."[33] (The Domestic and Indian Mission Board had changed its name to Home Mission Board in 1874.)

It is important to note that while far-reaching changes

were transforming American and Baptist life, and while the association's premier position as the denomination's arm of outreach was being usurped by the more recently formed Baptist entities, the associations still managed to maintain a healthy interest and participation in Indian missions. In 1851, Charleston Association had recorded in the minutes of its annual meeting:

Here, on our immediate borders, embracing that vast area of country extending from the Mississippi to the shores of the Pacific, are crowded those numerous tribes which have been gradually receding before the march of the white man. Here are the men whom we have driven from their homes—whose lands and whose rights we are now peacefully enjoying: they are perishing for want of the gospel, and their condition has been made more degrading and more wretched from contact with the very men who have deprived them of their homes and hunting grounds.

How inevitably the past intrudes itself into the future was indirectly alluded to in 1892 when Charleston and other associations published the Home Missions report relating to Indian work.

Work among these people is said to be hard . . . . Previous efforts with them have not yielded altogether encouraging results; but when we remember how treaties have been broken by the general government, how they have been driven from land to land by the same people who are now giving them the gospel of peace and love, . . . we should expect the work to be slow.

Such is the legacy of the "trail of tears." Any denomination or missionary who fails to gain an understanding of the historical background and the sociological factors involved will likely meet with failure in attempts to minister to Indians.

As Southern Baptist people moved into the West, Northwest, and Rocky Mountain areas, so did missions to the Indians. And Indian churches and associations have joined with the Home Mission Board in sending missionaries to the unevangelized tribes. As early as 1876, Charleston Association was proud to report in its annual minutes that "the Creeks have thirty-two churches, already organized into an association similar to ours."

But not all recently begun Indian work has been confined to tribes west of the Mississippi. In 1918, the Home Mission Board also turned its attention back toward the East. A mission among the Cherokees who escaped General Scott's dragnet was established in North Carolina. The same year saw work begun among another remnant, the Choctaws in Mississippi.[34] And in 1932, the Baptist Mission Association of Oklahoma began a work with the Seminoles of Florida. Through the years, that work has been supported by both the Home Mission Board and Miami Association of Florida.

Presently, the Home Mission Board, in cooperation with the various state conventions, the local associations, and the churches, ministers to every major tribe in our nation. A total of forty-eight missionaries serve in Indian work under appointment of the Home Mission Board.

But the centuries-old "Indian Problem" remains. While the 1970 census reported that 827,091 Indians were living in the United States, that total has undoubtedly climbed beyond one million. Indian population is increasing at several times the average population increase. Unfortunately, that increase has been accompanied by increased poverty. Unemployment rates on the Indian reservations averaged almost 40 percent in the mid 1970s. The median family income of the general population was $9,590 in 1970, while, for Indian families, it was only $5,832. Such statistics are solid evidence that the problem remains.[35]

Speculating about the future, Vine Deloria, a member of the Standing Rock Sioux tribe, and author of books intriguingly entitled *God Is Red, We Talk You Listen,* and *Custer Died for Your Sins,* has said: "Perhaps the only certainty is that Indians will continue to understand the conflict between Indians and the rest of society at its deepest level as a religious confrontation."[36] While one could wish to comprehend all that that statement means to Deloria, could it be that although the Indian author obviously is suggesting that the Indian Problem remains, and that it is just as much the problem of the rest of society, so must we realize the existence of opportunities for ministering in Christ's name exist?

Notes

1. Thurman Wilkins, *Cherokee Tragedy: The Story of the Ridge Family and the Decimation of a People* (New York: The Macmillan Company, 1970), Title.

2. Ralph W. Andrews, *Indian Leaders who helped Shape America* (Seattle: Superior Publishing Company, 1971), p. 88.

3. Henry Steele Commager, *Documents of American History* (New York: Appleton-Century-Crofts, 1963), p. 260.

4. Wilkins, p. 306.

5. Ibid., p. 307.

6. James Loren Belt, *Baptist Missions to the Indians of the Five Civilized Tribes of Oklahoma* (Unpublished Doctor's Dissertation, Central Baptist Seminary, 1955), pp. 22–38.

7. Wilkins, p. 315.

8. As quoted by Ola Elizabeth Winslow, *Master Roger Williams* (New York: Farrar, Straus & Giroux, 1973), p. 111.

9. James Kendall Hosmer, *Winthrop's Journal: History of New England, 1630–1649* (New York: Charles Scribners, 1908), p. 118.

10. Commager, p. 1.

11. As quoted in Dee Brown, *Bury My Heart at Wounded Knee* (New York: Holt, Rinehart & Winston, 1970), p. 2.

12. William Brandon, *The Last Americans: The Indian in American Culture* (New York: McGraw-Hill, 1974), p. 114.

13. Commager, p. 5.

14. Brandon, p. 10.

15. Commager, p. 18.

16. Brandon, pp. 190–191.

17. William Bradford, *History of Plymouth Plantation, 1620–1647* (Boston: Houghton Mifflin Company, 1912), pp. 25–26.

18. George Howe, "The Tragedy of King Philip," *American Heritage.* Dec. 1958, vol. 10, no. 1, pp. 65–80.

19. Perry Miller, *Roger Williams: His Contribution to the American Tradition* (New York: Atheneum, 1970), p. 20.

20. Ibid., p. 64.

21. Stephen Wright, *History of Shaftsbury Association* (Troy: A. G. Johnson, 1853), p. 81.

22. Stuart Ivison & Fred Rosser, *The Baptists in Upper and Lower Canada Before 1820* (Toronto: University of Toronto Press, 1956), p. 10.

23. Wright, p. 90.

24. Ibid., p. 104.

25. Ibid., p. 116.

26. *Encyclopedia of Southern Baptists,* "Indians, Home Missions to."

27. Belt, pp. 22–23.

28. Ibid., selected from pp. 25–98.

29. Ibid., pp. 58, 92.

30. *Encyclopedia of Southern Baptists, "American Indian Mission Association."*

31. *Encyclopedia of Southern Baptists,* "Indians, Home Missions to."

32. Belt, pp. 67, 114.

33. *Encyclopedia of Southern Baptists,* "Home Mission Board of the Southern Baptist Convention."

34. *Encyclopedia of Southern Baptists,* "Indians, Home Missions to."

35. 1970 Census Statistics, and Orrin D. Morris, "Racial and Ethnic Diversity," an address to associational directors of missions, Glorieta Baptist Conference Center, July 19, 1978.

36. Vine Deloria, *Current History,* Dec. 1974, vol. 67, no. 400, pp. 245–46.

8

THE ASSOCIATION AND THE WOMAN'S MISSIONARY MOVEMENT

*We commend to our churches the formation
of Woman's Missionary Societies to aid in this
work which none can do so well as woman.
Woman calls to woman, and looks to sisters
for a response of loving Christian devotion to
come to her relief. The call from foreign lands
is to you, Christian women and sisters of the
churches of this association.*

Minutes of Charleston Association, 1876

When the Mount Pisgah church sent a query to the 1817 annual meeting asking Charleston Association if it would "tend to promote the glory of God and the prosperity of Zion" for the association to appoint itinerant missionaries to minister to destitute churches, the association replied that it would; and Richard Furman reported that a "pious lady had put thirty dollars in his hand" for that purpose.

That simple event recorded in the minutes of Charleston Association was prophetic of the kind of missions support Baptists came to take for granted from their women. Elizabeth McNair was the pious lady, and she also gave the association $100 toward establishing a theological seminary. Two other ladies gave $15 to the Education Fund, and, in 1819, Mrs. Hepzibah Townsend contributed $60. Those ladies of Charleston Association, and others who shared their concerns in sister associations, were crucial strands in the warp and woof that wove the developing "woman's work" into the total SBC fabric. Before another century passed, and before they had won for themselves national suffrage, women would be sitting as messengers to the associations—before they were to the Southern Baptist Convention!

It was out of the peculiar climate of expectancy and anticipation that ushered in the nineteenth century that both opportunity and impetus for an organized woman's movement in the religious realm sprang, a movement that, from the perspective of Southern Baptists, culminated May 11, 1888, in the basement of the Broad Street Methodist Church of Richmond, Virginia.

The missionary consciousness which began to pervade American Baptists following Carey's commitment of his life to India was the catalyst that brought forth the movement's birth in the first decade of the nineteenth century—almost half a century before a corresponding movement in secular life publicly exhibited itself. When the secular manifestation came, it owed much to the woman's movement in the religious realm, in fact, it could be said to have issued from it. Many of the first militant feminists were schooled for their crusades by the Woman's Christian Temperance Union. Susan B. Anthony was a Quaker, and history's first Woman's Rights Convention was sponsored by Quakers and held in a Methodist church.

Beginning with 1800, when a combination of Baptist and Congregational women founded the Boston Female Society For Missionary Purposes, the woman's missionary movement can be followed as it wound its way through four cumulative phases, cumulative because one phase did not cease when the next began. Through them all, the Baptist association was the frequent forum and was never far in the background.

Female Mite Societies

The first phase was evidenced by the development of the female mite and cent societies. The association's role at both their inception and continuing development was crucial. It was an essential adjunct to the proliferation of those societies during the first quarter of the nineteenth century. They, in turn, were vital links in the evolutionary chain that led to Woman's Missionary Union three-quarters of a century later. Almost any associational annual from that era reveals the intimate relationship that existed between the female societies and the associations. Missions support was the intense interest of the women, and the associations became the frequent avenues through which their funds were channeled into the work.

The annual minutes of Warren Association reveal how the various New England societies funneled their funds into missions support through the association. That association's circular letter of 1808 was highly laudatory of the "Missionary Society," likely the Massachusetts Baptist Missionary Society which had been formed at Boston in 1802 and which had already sent several men as missionaries to the Indians along the northeastern edges of the Great Lakes and on into Upper and Lower Canada. The association minutes reported that "upwards of $420 have been received" from three female societies in Boston, and "from a Female Mite Society in Providence, there have been received $193 in two years past." A cent society in Haverhill had sent in $111.12 over the past two years. Another in Salem had contributed $130 during the same period. The association clerk was astounded. He wrote, "Thus have these Societies notwithstanding their recent establishment contributed upwards of nine hundred dollars!" He then added, "Reader! Go thou and do likewise!" Many women did.

It would be difficult to adequately assess, or exaggerate, the impact the Judsons (Ann, in particular) had on the evolving woman's missionary movement. Baptists across the land spoke of them in intimate and endearing terms. The 1820 minutes of Shaftsbury Association spoke affectionately of "the support of Dr. Judson and his heroic wife upon the distant and barbarous coast of Burmah." Notably, that same meeting was "greeted . . . by several letters from the Female Mite Societies for Missionary Purposes." Baptist women were supporting their counterpart across the ocean. In 1827, Shaftsbury Association sadly "Resolved, that the association express their sentiments of affection and sympathy with our beloved Brother Judson in the late affliction which he sustained in the death of his beloved wife."[1] Beloved she was. Adoniram Judson had lost his wife, and America's Baptists had lost a favorite sister.

Ann Hasseltine Judson had become a Christian when she was sixteen, married at twenty-two, sailed two weeks later to India, and spent the rest of her life in the Orient. She was thirty-seven when she died. Her legacy to world missions endures today. That legacy includes the opportunity for women to personally participate in the missions enterprise. Other heroines, sung and unsung, followed in her wake. Some sailed across the sea. Others labored in their societies at home to provide support. More than one hundred societies submitted reports to the 1817 Triennial Convention, and Luther Rice commented: "Indeed, the great numbers and rapid increase of these laudable Female institutions cannot fail to create emotions the most lively and gratifying."[2]

To name any of Ann Judson's spiritual successors is unfair to so many who remain unnamed. But circumstances provided some of them with unusual opportunities to marshall emotional involvement and material support in the churches and associations. Henrietta Hall Shuck was one successor. She was baptized when she was thirteen by Jeremiah Bell Jeter, who would become the first president of the Southern Baptist Foreign Mission Board. Reading the story of Ann Judson turned Henrietta toward missions. And, like Ann, two weeks after her wedding, she sailed for the Orient with a new husband—who was clothed in garments made by a Beulah, Virginia, sewing society. The date of their sailing was September 22, 1835, nine years after the death of Ann Judson and exactly five weeks before Henrietta's eighteenth birthday. Another nine years and Henrietta Shuck would be dead, giving birth in Hong Kong, at age twenty-seven.[3]

Other women on whom the nineteenth-century missions mantle rested included the early China missionaries: Eliza Jane Whilden who went there with her husband in 1848 and died two years later; Martha Foster Crawford who sailed with her husband in 1851; Lula Whilden whose forty-four years of service began in 1872; the Moon sisters, Edmonia and Charlotte (Lottie), who went in 1872 and 1873; and Nellie Pierce who arrived in 1891 to serve until 1936. Meanwhile, Anne Bagby went to Brazil with her husband in 1880 and spent fifty-seven years there. Katherine Cheavens served in Mexico from 1898 until 1929.

Special Projects

The second phase of the woman's missionary movement was characterized by women's support of special projects. That rather nebulous phase may best be illustrated as it focused itself through the activities of Ann Graves, one of those who stayed by the baggage. Robert A. Baker has called her an "unsung heroine in this remarkable story," while an acquaintance described her as being "literally possessed by the spirit of missions."[4] When one considers her accomplishments in gathering widespread support for the Chinese "Bible Women," that evaluation is easily accepted. Her son,

Rosewell Hobart Graves, was appointed to China in 1855. Several years after his service began in Canton, he related in letters home that Chinese custom prevented him from witnessing to the female population. The best he could do was to train the few Christian women in Canton to tell Bible stories to their friends. However, those women were hindered from doing so by the long hours they labored. If there were some way to provide for their support, they could witness more effectively. Ann prayerfully shared that need with her two sisters in 1864. One of them sent fifty dollars to Rosewell. That sum helped to employ "the first Bible woman in China to go from house to house with the gospel message."[5]

With that modest success in her own family, Ann Graves proceeded to organize on a more extensive scale. As she did so, she broke new ground in the woman's missionary movement. In 1867, she organized the Baptist Female Missionary Prayer Meeting in Baltimore for "the support of native Bible women belonging to the Canton mission." When the Southern Baptist Convention met in her own Baltimore church in 1868, Ann convened a meeting of the women in the church basement. One participant recalled that "she told the ladies that her son . . . could not enter the homes of the women, and she begged them to go home to their churches and organize societies to raise money to employ native Bible women."[6] It was historically significant to the woman's missionary movement that Ann Graves coupled her appeal for funds with one that women organize societies in their home churches.

The movement toward national organization accelerated in 1871 when Woman's Mission to Woman was founded, also in Baltimore, with Ann Graves in a leadership role. She was elected corresponding secretary. In the circular letter Ann mailed out, she wrote: "We now appeal to the women of our Baptist churches to sustain this mission by their prayers and contributions. It is not intended to interfere with the regular missionary collections or to solicit aid through public meetings." The suggestion was made that the women of each church organize "for prayer and the dissemination of missionary intelligence." Significantly, it was also suggested that each state organize a mission society.[7]

Ann Graves was a mother seeking to assist her son's ministry in China. But any evaluation of her efforts in his behalf must also recognize that she greatly influenced the larger undertaking, that of a convention-wide woman's missionary organization. Woman's Mission to Woman with its plan for branches in the different states, Mite Boxes, and regular meetings for prayer and sharing of missionary information pointed the way. Others would walk in it.

The influence of Woman's Mission to Woman was observable almost immediately in the Foreign Mission Report made to the Southern Baptist Convention in 1872, the year Lula Whilden sailed for China. The delegates were urged to organize female societies in their churches. The report commended "the plan adopted by women of Baltimore . . . where each family . . . is supplied with a mission box (which costs five to ten cents) and every member of the household contributes two cents a week."[8]

Central Committees

The third phase was initiated by the organization of state central committees and was culminated by the founding of Woman's Missionary Union. How much Ann Graves and Woman's Mission to Woman influenced the development of the central committees is difficult to assess. Certainly some of them were founded to more effectively support some special project, just as Woman's Mission to Woman focused on the Canton Mission. South Carolina is a typical example. Lula Whilden was the catalyst that brought about that state's central committee. Mrs. J. D. Chapman, in her manuscript, "Through the Years with the Baptist Women of South Carolina," described her as being "a modest, quiet little woman." Lula Whilden was born at Camden in the year of the Southern Baptist Convention's birth. Her parents, Bayfield and Eliza Whilden, took her to China when she was three years old. Although her mother died two years later, Lula had already been infected with China. Back in South Carolina where her education was obtained at Greenville Female College, she maintained her commitment to return to China. However, unmarried women were not appointed missionaries to China at the time. But in 1872, when the Foreign Mission Board commissioned her brother-in-law, Nicholas B. Williams, and her sister, Jumille, to serve in China, Lula was appointed to accompany them.

Two years later, when South Carolina Baptists organized a central committee headed by Martha McIntosh of the Welsh Neck church, its special project was to raise money to build a home in Canton for the Williamses and Lula Whilden, as well as to support the girl's school Lula had established. The central committee wrote to pastors and churches throughout the state requesting names of ladies with whom it could correspond. Although the project varied, that was the frequent pattern followed by the state central committees.

That the central committees were effective in organizing societies and in bringing the woman's missionary movement nearer convention-wide union is seen in the response of the two mission boards. By 1876, the Foreign Mission Board had organized central committees for women's work in most of the convention states. That agency's report to the associations in that year included a strong appeal for the support of women. The success of that appeal is reflected in the fact that, five years later, H. A. Tupper, Corresponding Secretary of the Foreign Mission Board, estimated that

500 women's missionary societies existed in the Southern Baptist Convention.[9]

The Home Mission Board also began to see the value of women's organizations and sought to share in their benefits. In 1877, the committee on woman's work for the Home Mission Board made the following appeal:

We rejoice that . . . in co-operating through various associations for the accomplishments of objects quite away from their doors . . . the Christian women of our own day are doing more than . . . women have done for Christ. It is well known that within the last four years they have become well organized and devoted fellow-helpers . . . of Foreign Missions. Their sympathies have been deeply enlisted in behalf of their heathen sisters. . . . But it is not within the knowledge of your committee that the women of our Southern Baptist churches are making any organized effort in the line of work pursued by our Home Mission Board. Yet surely the time has come when this department of Christian service, as well as every other, should be blessed with the special prayers and gifts and labors of our Marys and Joannas, our Dorcases, Phoebes and Priscillas.[10]

Results were immediate. Within the year, the Southern Baptist Convention's Committee on Woman's Work prepared an elaborate recommendation which was presented to the 1878 convention. The committee suggested that central committees be organized in each of the states, that their object be missionary education and the organization of women's missionary societies, and—in response to the Home Mission Board's appeal—that each society decide which field it wished to support, foreign or home. It is not lost on students of the woman's missionary movement that the committee also recommended that "these societies should be *auxiliary* to the State Conventions, or to the Southern Baptist Convention."[11] Southern Baptists did not wish to see their women paddle their own missionary canoes as their counterparts were doing in the North, where women sometimes appointed their own missionaries without regard to any other agency.

The Home Mission Board's success in getting a share of Baptist women's support is reflected in that body's report, which was both an admonition and commendation, to Charleston Association in 1885.

The women in our churches must not forget the work of Home Missions. They are interested in it, they are working for it. The Woman's Missionary Societies of this state are supporting Miss Maitie Cole and her Industrial School in New Orleans.[12]

Eliza Y. Hyde, City Missionary to Charleston and, in addition to Maitie Cole, another of the early unsung Home Mission heroines, also benefited from the South Carolina Central Committee's generosity. Eliza Hyde has received scant attention from Baptist historians, considering she broke new ground for the participation of women in home missions. She was the second woman appointed by the South Carolina board, and the first to serve for an extended period. Her yearning had been to join Lula Whilden in China. When poor health prevented her from going, Eliza began a ministry to the underprivileged children of Charleston in 1883. Her work was so effective that the South Carolina Central Committee invited her to serve as the first superintendent of the recently organized Sunbeam Bands. In 1891, she was appointed City Missionary by the State Mission Board. It should be noted that although the appointment came from the state board, she served as City Missionary for Charleston Association. Her labor in that capacity was reported upon regularly over the next two decades in the annual minutes of Charleston Association. The 1891 annual related that "she has labored efficiently." That she had labored is certain! She had worked with the women's missionary societies of the Cannon Street Chapel and of the Citadel Square mission. She had also directed the "Happy Sunbeams" of Cannon Street and the "Wm Carey Sunbeams" of Citadel Square. In 1892, when she was the only woman under appointment of the state mission board, Eliza reported 704 visits, 1,716 tracts distributed, twenty Bibles and twelve Testaments given out. She had also attended temperance meetings and handed out temperance literature. Eliza apparently did more than some wanted done. She was accused of spoiling the poor. Her response was, "Can we do less than the Master did?"[13] It was out of the Sunbeam Band that met in the yard of her Charleston home that Jane, Florence, and Frank Lide all surrendered to China missions. One writer commented on Eliza's thwarted ambition to join Lula Whilden in China: "In the providence of God one missionary was kept home. Three were inspired to take her place."[14]

Perhaps Eliza Hyde's greatest significance was that she ministered in Charleston in much the same way that Lula Whilden did in Canton. There was a growing awareness that children without Christ in either city were equally destitute. Part of the genius of the Baptist woman's missionary movement was in its concern for the missionary education and participation of children. As early as 1800, the children of First Baptist Church of Charleston had been involved in a Juvenile Missionary and Education Society in support of the Catawba Indians. And in 1808, Warren Association had declared: "Even children have been forward in offering their little gains to meliorate the moral condition of their brothers of the wilderness."[15] When the Woman's Missionary Union was founded in 1888, it was only the natural expression of what long had been practiced when the preamble asserted that women were "desirous of stimulating the missionary spirit and the grace of giving among women and children of the churches."[16]

When May 11, 1888, arrived, Southern Baptist women were ready. Sacrificial living on the part of Ann Judson, Henrietta Shuck, Lula Whilden, Lottie Moon, Eliza Hyde, and many others—plus sacrificial giving by thousands of women—brought the woman's missionary movement to the point of national organization. Thirty-two delegates from twelve states gathered in the basement of Richmond's Broad Street Methodist Church. In the months immediately preceding the meeting, Martha McIntosh distributed ten statements on "How May General Organization Help Us?" One of the statements declared that "a woman's organization is an institution specially adapted to reach the individual." The statement continued: "She has time, patience, tact, ingenuity, consecration, and a sense of values, . . . fitting her for the work. The unused forces of the church may be thus developed, utilizing much that would otherwise be wasting."

A second statement affirmed that children's work is a prominent feature of woman's general organization effort. She suggested that with women and children organized and educated for missions, the previous year's embarrassment, when women's societies had given only an average of one-and-a-half cents to foreign missions, could be avoided in the future. The value of organization was magnified further in Maryland. That state's highly organized women and children gave an average of thirty-seven cents to missions. With Annie Armstrong pushing for convention-wide organization without further delay, the resolution to organize easily carried when the vote was taken on May 14, 1888.[17]

Certain distinguishing characteristics of Southern Baptists' Woman's Missionary Union should be noted. First, it encompasses all missions under the umbrella of its support. Second, it is auxiliary to the Southern Baptist Convention, which means it is cooperative and supportive, not competitive and combative. Its two objectives, which were adopted in keeping with its pre-convention publicity, were "to distribute missionary information and stimulate effort," and "to secure the earnest systematic co-operation of women

and children in collecting and raising money for missions
. . . disclaiming all intention of independent actions."[18]

Back to the Associations

A further distinguishing characteristic of the Woman's
Missionary Union, which really constitutes a fourth phase
of the total woman's missionary movement, is that after
organizing in 1888, it turned back to the associations and
churches for continued growth. While the association had
provided a forum for discussion all along, the very nature
of the work, dependent as it was on local societies, demanded that the primary focus return to the association.
After all, it was from there that the initial emphasis on
the mite societies had come.

The experience of Virginia's Roanoke Association is typical, and enlightening. The associational annual of 1894 included "Minutes of the First Annual Session of the Woman's
Missionary Union." The women met August 15, 1894, the
second day of the association's annual meeting and declared
their organization to be auxiliary to the association. Ten
local societies were represented. The body resolved in its
preamble: "Whereas; we the women of the Woman's Missionary Societies of the churches of Roanoke Baptist Association are desirous of stimulating a missionary spirit and the
grace of giving among women and children of the churches,
and in aiding of collecting funds for missionary purposes
to be distributed by the boards of the Virginia Baptist General Association and the SBC." In agreement with the policy
of the convention-wide union, the Roanoke Association
Woman's Missionary Union was emphasizing its cooperative
relationship with other Baptist bodies.

The association annual of 1895 is even more enlightening.
Mrs. Frank S. Woodson, the state central committee's vice-
president for Roanoke Association explained how the national and state unions looked to the local congregations

for continued enlistment and enlargement. Mrs. Woodson, who was from Danville, Virginia—the same city in which resides the current president of the Woman's Missionary Union of the Southern Baptist Convention—explained: "In each state there is a Central Committee, which is auxiliary to the General Association (State Convention). This Central Committee has a vice-president for each association whose duty it is to organize Woman's Missionary Societies in the churches throughout her association." Serving in that capacity, Mrs. Woodson had been instrumental in forming nine new societies during the year. With vice-presidents who were appointed by the state central committees functioning in most associations, the woman's missionary movement continued to expand.

Sunbeam Bands, which, in the early days of WMU, referred to the total children's program, continued to be stressed by the associational organization. Mrs. Woodson admonished the 1895 meeting: "Wherever there is interest enough to maintain a Woman's Missionary Society it is earnestly hoped that some of those workers will inaugurate mission work among the young." The same emphasis was evident in Charleston Association where Eliza Hyde directed the work. The Charleston Association WMU organized in 1903. It was noted by the association clerk that the ladies met October 28 "as auxiliary to Charleston Association."

Complete minutes of the meetings were carried in the association annual beginning with 1904. One of the questions debated in 1909 at a round table discussion conducted by Mrs. Fryor was "Should we teach Sunbeams to pray in their meetings?" While the resolution of that question was not recorded, that serious attention was given to the children is apparent. Other topics considered were: How often officers should be elected? How often the local society should meet? How can we get attendance in the country societies? How can we develop unused talent? How can we make society meetings interesting? How can we awaken uninterested women in our churches? "Miss Etta Wilder urged the societies to observe the special days on our calendar." Enlistment was in October. There would be a Christmas Offering and Week of Prayer and Self-denial. Mrs. Hoge spoke on "Our End of the Rope," and, to conclude a program that sounds very contemporary, Mrs. Matthews sang "Go Home and Tell!"

Women did go home and tell. And in the telling, Baptist people were soon won over to their support, even most pastors who had opposed the organization of Woman's Missionary Union. Consequently, in 1915, Miss Nannie Sykes of Mountain Hill and Miss Ethel Copeland of Schoolfield were seated as delegates to Roanoke Association without a whimper from the stronger sex. At least, none were recorded by the association clerk. In 1916, both Mr. and Mrs. F. H. Altice were registered as delegates from Elba.[19] That same year, in Charleston Association, A. J. Nielson (not Mrs.) was still chairman of the Committee on Woman's Work, but Miss Callie Wells was a delegate from the Bethel church, and Mrs. J. T. E. Thornhill was a delegate from Summerville. So was Mr. J. T. E.[20] Meanwhile, the Southern Baptist Convention was still two years away from seating women, which, when one thinks about it, says something good about the direction of flow in Southern Baptist life.

Notes

1. Stephen Wright, *History of Shaftsbury Association* (Troy: A. G. Johnson, 1853), Minutes of 1820 and 1827.

2. *Encyclopedia of Southern Baptists*, "Judson, Ann Hasseltine," and "Woman's Missionary Union," p. 1507.

3. Ibid., "Shuck, Henrietta Hall."

4. Robert A. Baker, "Ann Graves," *The Quarterly Review,* vol. 37, no. 3, April, May, June, 1977, p. 21.

5. As quoted in ibid., p. 22.

6. Ibid., p. 23.

7. As quoted in ibid., p. 23.

8. *Encyclopedia of Southern Baptists,* "Woman's Missionary Union."

9. Ibid.

10. As quoted in ibid.

11. As quoted in ibid.

12. Minutes of Charleston Association, 1885.

13. Ibid., 1891–1895.

14. As quoted in Joe M. King, *A History of South Carolina Baptists* (Columbia: L. Bryan Company for the General Board of the South Carolina Baptist Convention, 1964), p. 264.

15. *Encyclopedia of Southern Baptists,* "Woman's Missionary Union."

16. As quoted in ibid.

17. Ibid.

18. Ibid.

19. Minutes of Roanoke Association, 1915, 1916.

20. Minutes of Charleston Association, 1916.

Part III
THE ASSOCIATION'S DIRECTOR OF MISSIONS

In my way to Mars-bluff, on the Peedee, I lodged at the ferryman's house. He observed that he believed I was a minister, and wished me to tell him of the best and shortest way to heaven. I told him that Christ was the best way; and that he must become experimentally acquainted with him, and believe in him, which was the hope of glory. That after he had obtained this, the shortest way, that I knew, would be to place himself in front of some army, in an engagement.

John Gano, Memoirs
circa 1755

Many Baptists do not know what the director of missions does or, for that matter, what the association does. To remedy that denominational shortcoming and to set the stage for bold mission during the remainder of this century, several hundred Baptists from a broad spectrum of convention life gathered at Ridgecrest, North Carolina, in May 1974, for the National Convocation on the Southern Baptist Association. It was the most significant such event since the previous decade's smaller, and less representative, Gulfshore Conference.

Fred B. Moseley left no doubt concerning the high priority with which the Home Mission Board regarded the convocation when, in his orientation address, he stated: "We are convened to consider the future of the Baptist association." Thirty-two study groups, consisting of approximately thirty participants each, considered sundry issues of interest to Baptist associations.

A frequently recurring theme, voiced by many of the study groups, was that the key to the association's contributions to the future is the person who occupies what is considered by most Baptists to be the top position in the associational structure. In 1975, Ben C. Fisher called him "one of the keys to Southern Baptist growth and prosperity."[1] Another writer had characterized him almost two decades earlier as being "a representative of all phases of denominational life."[2]

However that person ought to be characterized, the consensus reached by that cross section of denominational leadership gathered at Ridgecrest in 1974 was that he should have a new title. When he arrived at the Ridgecrest Convocation, he was designated in most associations as the superintendent of missions. Earlier, up until the Gulfshore Conference on Associational Missions in 1963, he had been called the associational missionary. But after Ridgecrest, he ought to be called the director of missions. That was one of the convocation's conclusions. Study Group 14, whose particular assignment was *The Role of the Director of Missions,* stated: "Director more nearly fits the wide variety of associations in the SBC constituency."

Although it was a new title, Baptist history affirms that it was not a new office, nor even one of modern origin. Five years before the Ridgecrest Convocation, E. C. Watson had written: "While the advent of the superintendent of associational missions as we know him is of fairly recent origin, his roots are deep in Baptist history." He added, "Many prototypes are found in the early work of Baptists in this country."[3]

The evolution of associationalism in both England and America lends credence to Watson's contention. At various times and in various places—with varying degrees of similarity to the person who holds the present-day position—those prototypes are scattered throughout Baptist history. They served with a bewildering assortment of titles: agent, apostle, field worker, general agent, general missionary, general evangelist, itinerant preacher, messenger, traveling preacher. Those and others were the titles by which they were called.

During much of the nineteenth century, the person in the missionary position was often called simply that, the missionary. And regardless of the Ridgecrest Convocation's conclusions, those directors of missions who are appointed by the Home Mission Board continue to bear that simple designation. The Certificate of Appointment presented them at their commissioning service calls them "A Missionary of the Home Mission Board of the Southern Baptist Convention."

Notes

1. Ben C. Fisher, "Don't Underestimate the Power of the Association," *The Southern Baptist Educator,* vol. 34, no. 4, March–April, 1975, Editorial.

2. *Encyclopedia of Southern Baptists,* "Missouri Associations."

3. E. C. Watson, *Superintendent of Missions for an Association* (Atlanta: Home Mission Board, SBC, 1969), p. 7.

9.
THE PERIOD OF THE PASTOR-MISSIONARY
(1650–1750)

The first prototypes of the present-day director of missions lived in Wales during the brief time of Cromwell's protectorate. Two examples of those first Welsh prototypes are referred to in the minutes of the association records of South Wales, dated 6–7 November 1650.

The brethren, seriously weighinge the great scarcity of such ministers as will soundly hould foorth the word of truth in Carmarthenshire, and the seasonable opportunity now offered, by the providence of God, for the probogation of truth in those partes, doe judge it convenient, that Brother David Davis shall henceforth endeavore to preach two first dayes of every 2 months, at Carmarthenshire or thereaboutes; and that Brother Myles doe preach there-aboutes, one first day of every 2 months."[1]

It is worth noting that Davis and Myles were considered to be ministers who would "soundly hould foorth the word of truth." Thirty pounds per year were "to be raysed by the churches (of the association) in equal portions . . . towards the maintenance of the ministry." Of significance to associationalism in America, many of the first Baptists in Rhode Island and Pennsylvania arrived in those colonies after having fled Wales following the Restoration of Charles II in 1660. John Myles, one of those first missionaries, was among them.

Most of those early prototypes are best described as having been pastor-missionaries. They received no official commission from their denomination. They took no extended journeys. What distinguished them from other pastors of their day was their commitment to build congregations "into the next towns" beyond the local church field. John Myles was one of the more prominent examples. He was an admirable forerunner for the present-day missionary. Cotton Mather, who was not known to lavish praise on dissenters, said of John Myles that he was one "of those persons whose names deserve to live in our book for their piety."[2]

As a twenty-three-year-old youth, Myles was preaching as an independent in Wales at the same time seven Particular Baptist churches convened in association fashion in London to compose what history refers to as the London Confession of 1644. Five years later, Myles went to London with Thomas Proud where both joined the Baptist church ministered to by William Consett and Edward Draper. A few months later, Myles and Proud returned to Wales and formed on October 1, 1649, what was certainly one of the first Baptist churches, and possibly the first, in Wales at Ilston, Glamorganshire. That church, with Myles as its pastor, developed practices that would also characterize Baptist work in the first Pennsylvania churches. The most striking practice, from the standpoint of missionary outreach, was that of forming multiple congregations. Myles was the pastor; and there was one church. Ilston was the center of worship. But the church also consisted of several other congregations which met at different places. Occasionally, they all came together to observe the ordinances.[3]

Although it can not be definitely established that Myles was influenced by associationalism which was then developing in London, it is known that he soon became the leader of sixteen ministers who formed an association-type relationship of five churches. Myles was named that association's delegate to a meeting which gathered in London in 1651. The relationship he sustained with the other pastors was similar to the one that exists today between a director of missions and the pastors of an association. It could be compared, also, perhaps not very adequately, to cases where the association moderator serves as missionary-moderator. A persuasive preacher, Myles' own congregation numbered more than 260 members in 1660.[4]

The experience of John Myles, who emigrated from Wales to New England where he founded the first Baptist church in Massachusetts, was not atypical. William Cathcart wrote that "the first churches in Wales . . . were missionary centers of wide-ranging activity." It was not unusual for them to have several scattered congregations. Of significance to New World associationalism, Cathcart added: "Much of the formative work in Rhode Island, New Jersey, Virginia, New York, Delaware and Pennsylvania was done by them."[5] A. H. Newman was another historian who wrote of "the prevailing Welsh element among Pennsylvania Baptists."[6]

Although it is not certain, John Myles was likely one of associationalism's links between London and Wales. He and those other Welsh Baptists who fled to America after 1660 definitely formed the link between Old and New World associationalism. British Baptists, such as Elias Keach, were also in that connectional chain. Philadelphia Association, which was formed by those immigrants in 1707, then became, for almost half a century—until other associations began to form—associationalism's single line of continuity with succeeding Baptist history in America.

If one were to single out one individual from Philadelphia Association's first decade to stand as a prototype for future associational missionaries, Abel Morgan would likely be the overwhelming choice. Elias Keach could challenge for that honor but was off the scene before the association was officially formed. Born in Wales in 1673 (the son of *Morgan ap Rhydderch ap Dafydd ap Gruffydd!*), Abel took as a surname his father's Christian name and thus became simply Abel Morgan. At an early age, he rose to prominence among Welsh Baptists who were numerous in the vicinity of Abergavenny. In 1711, he joined the emigration to Pennsylvania. Almost immediately upon his arrival in America, in 1712, although tragedy had struck at sea where he lost his wife and infant son, Morgan assumed leadership of the Lower Dublin Church and its satellite in Philadelphia.[7]

That early eighteenth-century pastor-missionary was soon doing things similar to what directors of missions do today. When a fellowship problem threatened to split the Middletown church, Abel Morgan helped repair the breach. He also reached out from the Lower Dublin church to plant new congregations. Of the three additional churches received into the association from the time of his arrival in 1712 until 1720, Morgan was the catalyst for them all. At Brandywine, he gathered fifteen Baptists together and constituted them into a church in 1715. When the Hopewell church was organized, also in 1715, it was ministered to "chiefly by Abel Morgan" and two others for the next six years. When Baptists, who had been members of the church at Rhydwilym, Wales—where his father had been pastor— came to Montgomery, it was Abel Morgan who "visited them, and preached to as many as came to hear."[8]

By the third decade of Philadelphia Association's existence, the Great Awakening had begun to overcome the spiritual lethargy in which colonials had been mired following New England's witchcraft craze. In 1729, the association reported "considerable additions the past year in several churches, and some in most."[9] In 1735, the association rejoiced to record: "To our great joy and comfort we find that large additions have been made this year to some churches, and some in every church belonging to this body."[10] Baptists were beginning to grow.

Notes

1. B. R. White (ed.), *Association Records of the Particular Baptists of England, Wales, and Ireland to 1660* (London: The Baptist Historical Society, 1971), South Wales Association, p. 3.

2. *Dictionary of American Biography,* "Myles, John."

3. See Frank H. Thomas, Jr., "The Influence of British and Welsh Baptists upon Pennsylvania-New Jersey Baptists until 1750," *The Quarterly Review,* vol. 36, no. 3, April–May–June, 1976, pp. 14–25 for a discussion of practices passed on from British and Welsh Baptists.

4. *Dictionary of National Biography,* "Myles, John."

5. William Cathcart, *The Baptist Encyclopedia* (Philadelphia: Louis H. Everts, 1881), vol. 2, p. 1228.

6. A. H. Newman, *A History of The Baptist Churches in The United States* (New York: The Christian Literature Co., 1898), p. 210.

7. *Dictionary of American Biography,* "Morgan, Abel."

8. A. D. Gillette (ed.), *Minutes of Philadelphia Baptist Association, 1707–1807* (Microfilm copy obtained from the Historical Commission, SBC), pp. 13–27, and *Dictionary of American Biography,* "Morgan, Abel."

9. Gillette, Minutes of Philadelphia Association, p. 29.

10. Ibid., p. 36.

10.
THE ERA OF THE LONG-DISTANCE ITINERANT
(1750–1800)

Historical eras, in the absence of cataclysmic events, seldom separate themselves into neat packages. Characteristics by which they are distinguished usually overlap. Such was the case relating to the evolving missionary office as Baptists moved from the period of the pastor-missionary into the era of the itinerant preacher.

In marked contrast to the denomination's past history, the man most representative of the era of long-distance itinerants, so designated to differentiate them from the next half-century's associational itinerants, neither was from Wales nor of Welsh descent. The dominant missionary figure from 1752, when Philadelphia Association sent itinerants south to Virginia for the first time, until his death in the first decade of the nineteenth century, was a short, slightly built great-grandson of French Huguenots who had escaped to America following the revocation of the Edict of Nantes. His name was John Gano.

He has been called the South's first associational missionary.[1] While that designation might be subject to dispute, that John Gano was a worthy prototype for future missionaries is not. He exhibited the same qualities expected of those who are appointed by our mission boards today. First, he experienced a genuine salvation experience, a fact that is apparent from his description of it in his memoirs. Second, he felt a strong sense of calling. "While on my knees," he wrote, "imploring the direction of God, these words powerfully impressed my mind: 'Go forth and preach the gospel.' " The tug of God's spirit would not turn loose. Gano related further: "One day I went early into the field, to plough it free from stumps and stones. Soon after I started, this text weighed heavy on my mind: 'Warn the people, or their blood will I require at your hands.' "[2] Third, he qualified himself mentally and, to the best of his limited ability in that day, academically. Gano studied under the tutelage of a Presbyterian minister and also attended classes informally at Princeton College. Fourth, he practiced missions before he was sent out by Philadelphia Association to serve in a missionary capacity. As pastor of the tiny Morristown church while in his mid-twenties, Gano extended his ministry in the fashion of a pastor-missionary to Baskinridge, Mendham, and Pasaic. At the same time, he explained, "I also visited Black-river, where there was a young and destitute church, which employed so much of my time, that my studies were much interrupted."[3]

In 1752, he became an itinerant missionary. That was when Philadelphia Association sent two teams of itinerants consisting of two men on each team to Virginia. John Gano quickly became the association's most widely traveled itinerant. His memoirs tell of weeks spent on horseback traveling down poorly defined roads and of nights spent on the floor of primitive cabins. During the French and Indian War, he was mistaken for a French spy and on other occasions was threatened with various acts of violence and robbery. On one trip from the Yadkin to South Carolina, he had "high waters to pass," not an infrequent experience for that day's itinerant preachers. An Anglican contemporary of Gano's, who served in the same area, described one of his missionary journeys as follows: "A shocking passage. Obliged to cut my way thro' the swamp for 4 miles, thro' canes and impenetrable woods—had my cloathes torn to pieces."[4]

It should be understood that John Gano stands simply

as a worthy symbol for future associational missionaries. He was not the only prototype who engaged in long-distance itinerancy during the eighteenth century. His companions on the first missionary journey to Virginia—Benjamin Miller of Scotch Plains, whom Gano described as being one of the most useful ministers of the day; John Thomas of Montgomery; and Isaac Sutton of Old Town—were others sent out on occasion from Philadelphia Association. Peter Peterson Vanhorn from the Lower Dublin church was another sometime itinerant for Philadelphia Association. Most served as part-time itinerants while pastoring at the same time.

Nor was Philadelphia Association the only possessor of prototypes for future associational missionaries. Shubal Stearns, Gano's contemporary, reached out from Sandy Creek in much the same fashion. David Benedict, whose source was Morgan Edwards, wrote of Stearns that he "often traveled a considerable distance in the country around, to assist in organizing and regulating the churches he and his associates were instrumental in raising up."[5] Daniel Marshall, also a Separate Baptist from Sandy Creek, traveled south to Georgia. And around the turn of the century, Richard Furman, while pastor of the First Baptist Church of Charleston, also did part-time itinerant work on the islands off the Carolina coast.

Notes

1. *Encyclopedia of Southern Baptists,* "Charleston, S. C., First Baptist Church."

2. John Gano, *Biographical Memoirs of the Late Rev. John Gano of Frankfort* (Kentucky), formerly of the City of New York, written principally by himself (New York: Southwicke and Hardcastle, 1806), pp. 31–34.

3. Ibid., p. 54.

4. Gano, pp. 36–69 for Gano's experiences, and Richard J. Hooker (ed.), *The Carolina Backcountry on the Eve of the Revolution* (Chapel Hill: University of North Carolina Press, 1953), p. 12.

5. David Benedict, *A General History of the Baptist Denomination in America and other Parts of the World* (New York: Lewis Colby and Co., 1848), p. 684.

11

THE AGE OF THE ASSOCIATION ITINERANT (1800–1845)

Charleston, South Carolina, is as logical a place as any with which to begin the account of the association itinerant. The nineteenth century opened with the country, and Baptists, growing both geographically and numerically. Five-and-one-third million citizens were spread from the Atlantic westward to the Mississippi. By 1810, the number had increased to more than seven and one-quarter million. Approximately 3 percent of them held membership in about 2,500 Baptist churches, which were affiliated with upwards of 100 associations.[1] Having reached such dimensions, no longer could a single individual serve as an adequate symbol for any aspect of denominational activity. But Charleston could serve as a typical association. Organized in 1751, second association in America, it probably exerted greater influence on the early development of the Southern Baptist Convention than did any other association.

What is observable in the various association minutes of the age is that the nature of itinerant work had begun to change even before the turn of the century. While the first itinerants were few and often conducted their ministries far from sponsoring associations, nineteenth-century itinerants would be more numerous, and the emphasis would be shifted nearer home.

Charleston Association, as early as 1779, had established a standing committee to transact business between annual meetings, much as the association executive board does in the interim today. One of that committee's duties was to "recommend traveling ministers of good character."[2] Other associations acted accordingly. A committee of Virginia's Roanoke Association recommended in 1789 "that vacant churches, or churches destitute of ministers, be considered by the association, and that the same be supplied from time to time, by ministers in rotation." Both Charleston and Roanoke associations were thinking of ministries within their own areas. Roanoke Association appointed five pastors, one of whom was Samuel Harris, "to supply the church at Bannister."[3] The quality of the men selected is reflected in the fact that Harris, "the Apostle of Virginia," had organized numerous churches and had long been one of the most influential Baptists in Virginia.

Ironically, it was the foreign missions movement that forced the associations to place greater emphasis upon nearby mission opportunities. Popularization of William Carey's mission to India led to the proliferation of numerous mission societies during the nineteenth-century's first decade. The Triennial Convention, which was really a foreign mission society that was national in scope, was founded in 1814. Luther Rice was soon crisscrossing the country to raise funds in the convention's behalf to support the Judson's in Burma. While few today would question the value of Rice's contributions, the short-term result was that mission interests of Baptists were focused overwhelmingly on needs in exotic lands, to the detriment of needs at home.

The associations began to counter that unbalanced tilt toward "Burmah." A query was addressed to the 1817 annual meeting of Charleston Association asking: "Would it not tend to promote the glory of God and the prosperity of zion for this association to appoint ministers to itinerate and preach among our destitute churches and settlements in the state, which have not a standing ministry?" Other associations were being asked similar questions. Charleston Association decided it would "promote the glory of God and the prosperity of zion," and a committee was established "to devise a plan for attaining the object contemplated in the query."

The response was immediate and enthusiastic. The next annual meeting could report that $500 had been received into the Itinerant Fund, and the association adopted significant guidelines to govern its use. Those guidelines set out by Charleston Association, along with similar ones established earlier by New England's Shaftsbury Association, helped point Baptists toward that age's pressing need for home missions.

"Rules for establishing a scheme of itinerant preaching for home missions"—that was what the association minutes of 1818 called the guidelines. First, there was to be a Board of Directors composed of five members, including a chairman, treasurer, and secretary. Those selected were to be "of the most enlightened and public spirited members of the churches in this connexion." Second, when the Itinerant Fund was sufficient, "the Board shall be authorized to appoint a person, or persons, to itinerate, and preach among Destitute Churches and settlements in this state." Denoting the importance attached to the projected itinerant ministry, the board was to appoint "only preachers of approved character, distinguished for their prudence, piety, and zeal, and of respectable talents." Each appointee was presented with a certificate of appointment and with written instructions to guide him in his conduct. In further elaboration, those appointed as association itinerants were to refrain from contentions with those of other denominations. They were to preach "among the people at large . . . on the most plain, important . . . truths of the gospel, with a view to the conversion of sinners and the regular formation of churches." They were also to "enquire into the state of destitute churches, and afford them aid, in removing difficulties, and rectifying disorders."

At the next annual meeting in 1819, it was reported that a Mr. Walke had been employed as an "Itinerant Preacher" under the board's direction. He had preached among the destitute in various parts of the state, and "favorable accounts had been received of his acceptance, and the usefulness of his labors." Two years later "the Domestic Mission was of such magnitude" that two missionaries were employed. By 1825 three were at work. One, a Brother Rollins, had baptized forty-five converts.[4]

Refinements began to be made in the associational missions program, refinements that moved it in the direction of today's practices. Charleston Association began to designate a specific territory to each itinerant preacher. In 1828, Brother Rollins was appointed to "the neighborhood of the Pee Dee," and Brother Burnett to "a very destitute tract of country below the Santee."[5] By 1837, the association could report that "the Home Mission Board (meaning the Charleston Association board) have laid out . . . definite circuits for their missionaries, and given them such instructions as deemed expedient."[6]

Notes

1. Gordon Carruth (ed.), *The Encyclopedia of American Facts & Dates* (New York: Thomas Y. Crowell Co., 1970) gives population statistics for 1800 as 5,308,483 and for 1810 as 7,239,881; Benedict, *A General History,* p. 366 gives Baptist statistics for 1812 as 204,185 members, 2,633 churches, 111 associations.

2. *Encyclopedia of Southern Baptists,* "Itinerancy, Southern Baptist Ministers."

3. Minutes of Roanoke Association, 1789.

4. Minutes of Charleston Association, 1819, 1821, and 1825.

5. Ibid., 1828.

6. Ibid., 1837.

12.
ALMOST A CENTURY OF SOUTHERN BAPTIST EXPERIMENTATION (1845–1940)

"Unanimously Resolved, That the association approve of the separation of the Southern churches from the Northern, and the formation of the Southern Baptist Convention."[1]

Resolutions similar to that were adopted in scores of associations in the fall of 1845, aftermath of action by Baptists of the South the past May at Augusta, Georgia. Statistics for the Southern Baptist Convention's first year reported 351,951 members in 4,126 churches. That was almost one-half of the country's mainline Baptists.

For those churches and the associations they constituted, it would become more than a new affiliation. It would initiate a time of experimentation, a time of searching for new and better ways in all phases of denominational activity, including their conduct of associational missions. It was the beginning of what turned out to be almost a century of experimentation, as well as a time of trauma. The office of associational missionary would become one laboratory for experimentation.

As the new convention struggled to find its place of ministry, it was determined to avoid what were considered to be the inequities of their past denominational affiliation. A contributing factor in bringing about the formation of the Southern Baptist Convention had been the prevalent complaint of southerners that the homeland, especially their part of it, had been slighted in the outlay of mission resources. To correct that in its own ministry, new methods in missions outreach were among the first experiments undertaken by the convention, and the missionaries were among the first affected.

One new method, which would significantly alter previous mission practices, as well as give form to future ones, began to take shape almost immediately. It involved cooperative agreements (although they were not called that) between the associations and the Domestic Mission Board. Charleston Association passed the following resolution in 1847: "That the two missionary boards heretofore connected with this association be discontinued. . . . That a (new) Missionary Board be composed of seven members of this association, be annually appointed, to which Board shall be committed the direction of missionary operations within the bounds of this body." The new board was instructed to "correspond with the Domestic Missionary Board located at Marion, Alabama (the first headquarters of what is now the Home Mission Board); and if deemed desirable to enter into an arrangement with said Board to supply with missionary efforts the destitute portions of our associational district."[2]

To enter into that arrangement was "deemed desirable" by Charleston Association, and the new associational missions board was pleased to report to the next annual meeting in 1848 that it had "effected satisfactory arrangements with the Marion Board, by which we were to become auxiliary to that board." To allay any fears such apparent surrender of associational autonomy might have aroused, the association hastened to assure that it would continue to appoint and control its own missionaries with pay to be provided by the association, but "supplemented as necessary from Marion." The report continued: "Under this organization, we recommended to the Marion Board to appoint the Rev. Joseph A. Lawton Missionary to Charleston Neck, the Rev. H. A. Duncan for Columbia, the Rev. J. H. Pearson for South Santee, the Rev. Thomas Dawson for North Santee."

Significant to future decades, what had been neg
between the association and the Domestic Mission
was an early experiment with cooperative agree
Even the reports from that day's missionaries have a contemporary ring. Thomas Dawson reported that, in 1848,
he had preached ninety-four sermons, delivered twenty-
nine evening lectures, made 154 visits, and traveled 1,400
miles. Further explanation was made that "he occupied 18
regular stations, and preaches every day. He has spent a
good deal of his time in resuscitating and building up feeble
churches." With the kind of mixed adjectives that describe
some present-day associations, the report concluded, "His
field is large, destitute, and full of promise."[3]

The Civil War interrupted Southern Baptists' nineteenth-
century bold mission thrust. Its impact was traumatic. The
objectives of the SBC had been bold for its age. Two objectives had been magnified in 1851: one, to assist feeble
churches throughout the southern and southwestern states
and territories to "obtain the stated preaching of the gospel"; and, two, "to supply newly settled and growing parts
of the country with the preaching of the gospel where we
have at present no churches."[4] The new convention had
no intention of becoming provincial. The nation was its
field, and progress was being made.

It was in April 1861 that the South's dream began to
shatter at Charleston, South Carolina, in Beauregard's bom-
bardment of Fort Sumter. That was followed by the first
Battle of Bull Run three months later. Although the early
encounters resulted in southern victories, Rhett Butler was
not alone in believing the ultimate end spelled disaster for
the South.

Mission activities were inhibited almost immediately. As
the war worsened for the South, retrenchment became the
order of the day for Southern Baptists. Work on the West
Coast was terminated. The Domestic Board's missionary

force declined from 159 in 1860 to 32 three years later.[5] When the conflict ended in 1865, what funds were available to the Domestic Mission Board were Confederate. It, like the South, was bankrupt.

Recovery from the debacle was complicated by Reconstruction and required two decades. Seventeen years after Appomattox, Southern Baptists were still fragmented. Some of the southern states were cooperating with the American Baptist Home Mission Society. Texas was ridden with internal strife. Elsewhere west of the Mississippi, there was little Southern Baptist witness.

The association's response during this time of crisis was often one of increased reliance on Baptist agencies beyond itself. Charleston Association suggested in 1875 "that the time has come when our mission work should be performed through the State Board."[6]

Perhaps it was the frequent grasping for new handles which accompanied those trying times that brought a new phraseology into the Baptist vocabulary. The titles by which the missionaries were called is indicative of the state of flux that existed. Some continued simply to be missionaries. But agents were also employed. From that came general agents and general missionaries, both of which designations were applied to Joseph Warner Dossey Creath by the Texas convention. Other titles for those persons who stand in the general lineage of present-day directors of missions, which soon found their way into the convention lexicon, were colporteur, colporteur and missionary, and general evangelist.

With Isaac Taylor Tichenor's term as Secretary of the Home Mission Board, which began in 1882, the South began to rise again. Ten years later, the SBC annual reported that "its territory had been reclaimed."[7] A new spirit of optimism pervaded Southern Baptists. During that decade, church membership had increased by 44 percent to total

1,321,540 Southern Baptists. The number of churches cooperating with the convention had grown by 32 percent to total 17,710.[8]

The return of good times and the beginning of the twentieth century brought no lessening of either experimentation or cooperative missions. Early in the first decade, the Home Mission Board divided its work into five areas of responsibility—Mountain, Frontier, Ports of Immigration, Cooperative Missions, and Church Building and Missionary labor in Cuba. Along with the new mission structures, new titles were added for those in the long line of missionary prototypes that then stretched across two-and-one-half centuries. For example, A. J. Neilson was State Superintendent of City Missions to Charleston Association in 1913.[9] T. Ryland Sanford suggested to Virginia's Roanoke Association in 1921 that it "employ a Field Worker, whose duties it shall be to cooperate with all pastorless churches, . . . assisting in the forming of compact fields . . . the locating of pastors, holding Sunday School and B.Y.P.U. Institutes whenever advisable."[10]

Notes

1. Minutes of Charleston Association, ibid., 1845.
2. Ibid., 1847.
3. Ibid.
4. As quoted in Arthur B. Rutledge, *Mission to America* (Nashville: Broadman Press, 1969), p. 20.
5. Ibid., p. 30.
6. Minutes of Charleston Association, 1875.
7. *Encyclopedia of Southern Baptists*, "Southern Baptist Convention, The."
8. "Southern Baptist Summary," *The Quarterly Reveiw,* vol. 35, no. 4, July–August–September, 1975, pp. 70–71. (Repeated each year on the same pages of that periodical.)
9. Minutes of Charleston Association, 1913.
10. Minutes of Roanoke Association, 1921.

13

THE PRESENT AGE OF ASSOCIATIONAL ADVANCE (1940—PRESENT)

As the Southern Baptist Convention moved through the first decades of the twentieth century toward the present era, which dates from 1940, it did so with optimism. The Home Mission Board's sizable debt, which limited its activities during the twenties and thirties, and the decade-long depression which began in 1929 were considerable exceptions. However, those years of despair saw baptisms, Sunday School enrollment, and church membership continue upward trends. From the beginning of the century until 1940, there had been a net gain of one church for every two-and-a-half days. That statistic is even more impressive when one learns that upwards of 3,000 BMA churches were dropped in the mid-twenties. Membership in Southern Baptist churches had climbed from 1,657,996 in 1900 to 5,104,327 in 1940.[1]

By 1940, with both the depression and the Home Mission Board's debt finally in hand, Southern Baptists were prepared to move into the present age of associational advance. New mission structures would be organized within the Home Mission Board. New outreach strategies would be devised. Accompanying this would be a significant renewal of emphasis on the association as the key unit, beyond the local church in Baptist life. One writer would argue that the association was the keystone of all missions.

All facts of the forties are shrouded in that decade's single overwhelming fact, which was World War II. Unrelated and less significant events tend to be forgotten. But it was exactly thirteen months before Pearl Harbor plunged America into the conflict that the modern Home Mission Board program of city missions was authorized. The board met November 7, 1940, and "Resolved that the Executive Secretary be instructed to project a city missions program looking to the establishment of city missions in the South as funds shall be provided."[2] Southern Baptists, although predominantly a rural oriented people, from their foundation have discerned the strategic wisdom of capturing the metropolitan centers for Christ. Mission work in New Orleans had been authorized at the time of the convention's organization. Other city ministries had been instituted prior to the Civil War at Montgomery, Richmond, Augusta, San Francisco, Sacramento, and Oakland.

The resolution of November 7, 1940, was implemented when two programs began to function in February, 1941. Loyd Corder was appointed Superintendent of City Missions in Houston, and S. F. Dowis was appointed to serve in the same capacity in Atlanta. By the end of 1943, twenty-one cities were participating in the program. The ministries were cooperative, involving the Home Mission Board and the associations. State Conventions were included in the cooperative agreements in 1951.[3] Today, about 275 metropolitan areas, which by definition are centers of population above 50,000, are being ministered to by associational directors of missions who relate to the Department of Metropolitan Missions of the Home Mission Board.

While a rural associational emphasis had also been called for prior to the nation's entry into World War II, the implementation of it began in 1943 under the direction of Courts Redford. A Rural Department was established in 1946 and in 1947 was placed under the supervision of the Cooperative Missions Department. The program called for a superintendent of missions in each state and an associational missionary in each association. Almost three-fourth's of the

1,200 associations in the Southern Baptist Convention are rural-urban in character.

The renewed focus on the association in Baptist life has been accompanied by a return of the associational missionary, by whatever title, to a place of respect and influence in the denomination. Various charges leveled against the associational missionary in the early stages of the present era, even to the point of questioning his right to exist, had usurped his influence. Most of those charges proved to be frivolous and have long since been silenced. Praises showered upon the director of missions by various authors during the last two decades are generally accepted today.

Harold D. Gregory forcefully contended in 1949, when criticisms were in vogue, that an association missions program directed by a missionary paid dividends in evangelism, in the formation of new churches, in more efficient education work, and in more mission involvement.[4] Twenty years later, E. C. Watson was even more definitive in outlining eight benefits that accrue to the association which has a missionary.[5] Merle A. Mitchell, who wrote the article on Missouri associations for the *Encyclopedia of Southern Baptists* characterized the associational missionary as: "A combined denominational administrator and a servant of the churches. . . . A representative of all phases of denominational life, a promotional secretary, a pastor at large, an associate to pastors, and a pastor to pastors." Mitchell noted that the missionary coordinates the work of the association among the churches and suggested that the work's success was owing largely to the missionary.[6] Ben C. Fisher made essentially the same point in 1975 when he editorialized: "One of the keys to Southern Baptist growth and prosperity has been the emergence of strong leadership in the form of the associational missionary or director of missions."[7] Finally, directors of missions will not forget that two great convocations influenced the enhanced esteem with which

179

their office is presently honored. Those were the National Convocation on the Southern Baptist Association at Ridgecrest, North Carolina, in 1974 and the previous decade's Gulfshore Conference. Both resulted in new names for the missionary office. Also Gulfshore clarified the role of the missionary, while Ridgecrest clarified the place of the association itself in relation to other denominational entities.

Pastor-missionary, itinerant preacher, associational missionary, superintendent of missions, directors of missions—that is where the evolution of the missionary office has arrived today. Those Welsh prototypes might be amazed at what three and one-quarter centuries have brought to the position. But the more amazing thing is that they could still recognize and identify with it.

Notes

1. "Southern Baptist Summary," *The Quarterly Review*, any July–August–September issue, pp. 70–71.
2. *Encyclopedia of Southern Baptists*, "City Missions."
3. Ibid.
4. Harold D. Gregory, *Local Missions: Keystone to All Missions* (Nashville: Executive Board, Tennessee Baptist Convention, 1949), pp. 154–159.
5. Watson, pp. 22–25.
6. *Encyclopedia of Southern Baptists*, "Missouri Associations."
7. Fisher, see note 1, p. 155.

Bibliography

ALDEN, JOHN R. *A History of The American Revolution.* New York: Alfred A. Knopf, Inc., 1969.

ALLEY, REUBEN EDWARD. *A History of Baptists in Virginia.* Richmond: Virginia Baptist General Board, 1974.

BABCOCK, RUFUS. *Forty Years of Pioneer Life:* Memoir of John Mason Peck. Carbondale: Southern Illinois University Press, 1965.

BACKUS, ISAAC. *A History of New England with Particular Reference to the Baptists.* Microprint copy at the University of California, Riverside.

BAILYN, BERNARD. *The Ideological Origins of The American Revolution.* Cambridge: Harvard University Press, 1967.

BAKER, ROBERT A. *The Blossoming Desert.* Waco: Word Books, 1970.

_____. *The Southern Baptist Convention and Its People, 1607–1972.* Nashville: Broadman Press, 1974.

BARNES, WILLIAM WRIGHT. *The Southern Baptist Convention, A Study in the Development of Ecclesiology.* Published by the author, Seminary Hill, Texas, 1934.

_____. *The Southern Baptist Convention, 1845–1953.* Nashville: Broadman Press, 1954.

BELT, JAMES LOREN. *Baptist Missions to the Indians of the Five Civilized Tribes of Oklahoma.* Doctors Dissertation, Central Baptist Seminary, 1955.

BENEDICT, DAVID. *A General History of the Baptist Denomination in America and Other Parts of the World.* New York: Lewis Colby and Co., 1848.

BENNETT, F. RUSSELL, JR. *The Fellowship of Kindred Minds.* Atlanta: Home Mission Board of the SBC, 1974.

BILLINGTON, RAY ALLEN. *Westward Expansion—A History of the American Frontier.* New York: Macmillan Publishing Co., Inc., 1974.

BRADFORD, WILLIAM. *History of Plymouth Plantation, 1620–1647.* Boston: Houghton Mifflin Company, 1912.

BRANDON, WILLIAM. *The Last Americans:* The Indian in American Culture. New York: McGraw-Hill, 1974.

BROWN, DEE. *Bury My Heart at Wounded Knee.* New York: Holt, Rinehart & Winston, 1970.

CATHCART, WILLIAM. *The Baptist Encyclopedia.* Philadelphia: Louis H. Everts, 1881.

COMMAGER, HENRY STEELE. *Documents of American History.* New York: Appleton-Century-Crofts, 1963.

COX, NORMAN W., ed. *Encyclopedia of Southern Baptists,* 3 Vols. I and II Nashville: Broadman Press, 1958; Davis C. Woolley, ed., Vol. III. Nashville: Broadman Press, 1971.

FORD, GLYNN Roland. *The Baptist District Associations of Virginia, 1766–1950.* Dissertation: Southern Baptist Theological Seminary, 1961.

GANO, JOHN. *Biographical Memoirs of the Late Rev. John Gano of Frankfort.* New York: Southwicke and Hardcastle, 1806.

GILLETTE, A. D., ed. *Minutes of Philadelphia Baptist Association, 1707–1807.* Microfilm obtained from The Historical Commission, SBC.

GREGORY, HAROLD D. *Local Missions: Keystone to All Missions.* Nashville: Executive Board, Tennessee Baptist Convention, 1949.

GUTHMAN, WILLIAM H. *March to Massacre: A History of the First Seven Years of the United States Army, 1784–1791.* New York: McGraw Hill Book Company, 1970.

HARVEY, SAM. *The Southern Baptist Contribution to the Baptist Cause in California Prior to 1890.* Thesis: Golden Gate Baptist Theological Seminary, 1958.

HOOKER, RICHARD J., ed. *The Carolina Backcountry on the Eve of the Revolution.* Chapel Hill: University of North Carolina Press, 1953.

HOSMER, JAMES KENDALL, ed. *Winthrop's Journal: History of New England, 1630–1649.* New York: Charles Scribner's, 1908.

HOVEY, ALVAH. *The Life and Times of the Rev. Isaac Backus.* Boston: Gould and Lincoln, 1858.

HUGGINS, M. A. *A History of North Carolina Baptists, 1727–1932.* Raleigh: The General Board, Baptist State Convention of North Carolina, 1967.

IVISON, STUART & ROSSER, FRED. *The Baptists in Upper and Lower Canada Before 1820.* Toronto: University of Toronto Press, 1956.

KINCAID, ROBERT L. *The Wilderness Road.* Indianapolis-New York: The Bobbs-Merrill Company, 1947.

KING, JOE M. *A History of South Carolina Baptists.* Columbia:

L. Bryan Company, General Board of the South Carolina Baptist Convention, 1964.

LOONEY, FLOYD. *History of California Southern Baptists.* Fresno: The Southern Baptist General Convention of California, 1954.

LUMPKIN, WILLIAM L. Baptist Confessions of Faith. Philadelphia: The Judson Press, 1959.

_____. *Baptist Foundations in the South.* Nashville: Broadman Press, 1961.

MCGLOTHLIN, W. J. *Baptist Confessions of Faith.* Philadelphia: American Baptist Publication Society.

MCLOUGHLIN, WILLIAM G. *Isaac Backus and The American Pietistic Tradition.* Boston: Little, Brown, and Company, 1967.

_____. *Isaac Backus on Church, State, and Calvinism—Pamphlets, 1754–1789.* Cambridge: Harvard University Press, 1968.

_____. *New England Dissent, 1630–1833:* The Baptists and Separation of Church and State. 2 vols. Cambridge: Harvard University Press, 1971.

MILLER, PERRY. *Roger Williams: His Contribution to the American Tradition.* New York: Atheneum, 1970.

NEWMAN, A. H. *A History of the Baptist Churches in the United States.* New York: The Christian Literature Co., 1898.

_____. *A Manual of Church History.* Philadelphia: American Baptist Publication Society, 1912.

PETERSON, MERRILL D., ed. *The Founding Fathers: James Madison, A Biography in His Own Words.* New York: Harper & Row, 1974.

POSEY, WALTER BROWNLOW. *The Baptist Church in the Lower Mississippi Valley, 1776–1845.* University of Kentucky Press, 1957.

PROCTOR, EMERSON. *Georgia Baptists, Organization and Division: 1772–1840.* Thesis: Georgia Southern University, 1969.

RUTLEDGE, ARTHUR B. *Mission to America.* Nashville: Broadman Press, 1969.

RYLAND, GARNETT. *The Baptists of Virginia, 1699–1926.* Richmond: The Virginia Baptist Board of Missions and Education, 1955.

SEMPLE, ROBERT B. *A History of the Rise and Progress of Baptists in Virginia.* Richmond: Pitt & Dickinson, 1894.

SHURDEN, WALTER B. *Associationalism Among Baptists in America, 1707–1814.* Dissertation: New Orleans Baptist Theological Seminary, 1967.

183

SWEET, WILLIAM WARREN. *Religion on the American Frontier: The Baptists, 1783–1830.* New York: Cooper Square Publishing, Inc., 1964.

_____. *The Story of Religion in America.* Grand Rapids: Baker Book House, 1973.

TAYLOR, JAMES B. *Memoir of Rev. Luther Rice.* Nashville: Broadman Press, 1937. Reprinted from 1841 edition.

TOWNSEND, LEAH. *South Carolina Baptists, 1670–1805.* Baltimore: Geneological Publishing Co., Inc., 1974.

WAMBLE, G. HUGH. *The Concept and Practice of Christian Fellowship: The Connectional and Inter-Denominational Aspects Thereof, Among Seventeenth Century English Baptists.* Dissertation: Southern Baptist Theological Seminary, 1955.

WATSON, E. C. *Superintendent of Missions for an Association.* Atlanta: Home Mission Board, SBC, 1969.

WHITE, B. R., ed. *Association Records of the Particular Baptists of England, Wales, and Ireland to 1660.* London: The Baptist Historical Society, 1971.

WHITLEY, W. T., ed. *Minutes of the General Baptist Churches in England, 1654–1728.* London: Kingsgate Press, 1909.

WILKINS, THURMAN. *Cherokee Tragedy: The Story of the Ridge Family and the Decimation of a People.* New York: The Macmillan Company, 1970.

WRIGHT, STEPHEN. *History of Shaftsbury Association.* Troy: A. G. Johnson, Steam Press Printers, 1853.

INDEX

Abergavenny, Wales, 160

Abingdon Association. *See Associations, Baptist*

Alamance, Battle of, 37, 46

Alamo, The, 57

Albemarle Association. *See Associations, Baptist*

Allegheny Mountains, 44, 52

Altice, F. H., 149

Altice, Mrs. F. H., 149

American Baptist Home Mission Society, 58, 59, 60, 174

American Baptist Publication Society, 59

American Board of Commissioners for Foreign Missions, 111

American Indian Mission Association. *See Associations, Baptist*

Anabaptists, 24

Anderson, Texas, 58

Annual Meeting, Lord's Supper at, 85–86

   Separate Baptists, reason for growth of, 38–39

   Significance of, 69–71

Anthony, Susan B., 136

Apache Indians, 121

"Apostle of Virginia," 168

"Apostle to the Indians" (Eliot, John), 123, 124

Appalachian Mountains, 45

Appleseed, Johnny (Chapman, John), 53

Armstrong, Annie, 146

Ashfield, Massachusetts, 97–98

Associations, Baptist

   Abingdon, baptism, advice concerning, 83

   first association, Baptist, 23

   organization of, 75

   Albemarle, Lord's Supper, observance of, 86

   American Indian Mission, organization of, 128–129

   Baptist Mission, work with Seminole Indians, 131

   Bethel, organization of, 53

   Charleston

      aiding the proliferation of Baptists, 18

      annual meeting, date of, 69

      Creek churches, report concerning, 130, 131

   Domestic Mission Board, resolution to cooperate with, 172

   education, Rhode Island College, support of, 79–80

   Heathen, prayer for, 110

   home missions, prayer for women's support of, 144

   itinerant missionaries, as a typical association using, 167–168

   itinerant missions, growth and refinements in, 170

   missionary, guidelines of, 169

   missionary outreach to Indians, 127

   missionary, reports of, 173

   ordination, advice concerning, 87–89

   queries to, 109, 135

   reliance on the state convention, 174

   Rice, Luther, visit of, 113

   slavery, defense of, 92

   Southern Baptist Convention, formation, resolution approving of, 171

   Woman's Missionary Union in, 148–149

   women delegates, seating of, 149

   work with Indians, opportunities and difficulty of, 130–131

Cherokee, organization of, 122

Choctaw-Chickasaw, organization of, 129

Congaree, organization of, 39

Coosa, in support of Indian missions, 129

Dover, baptism, conclusions concerning, 84

Ebenezeer, outreach to Indians, 128

Elkhorn

   Gano, John, chosen moderator of, 50

   Gano, John, mourning death of, 53

   organization of, 52

   slavery, discussion of, 91

General Association of Separate Baptists

   organization of, 39

   petition for religious freedom, 102

Georgia, associational power, limitations of, 75

Goshen

   missionary opportunities, 114

   in support of California work, 59

Holston, organization of, 52